**Cardiff Libraries**
www.cardiff.gov.uk/libraries

**Llyfrgelloedd Caerdydd**
www.caerdydd.gov.uk/llyfrgelloedd

D1140174

# Researching your Family History Online

**Prentice Hall**
is an imprint of

Harlow, England • London • New York • ... ...ore • Hong Kong
Tokyo • Seoul • Taipei • New Delhi • Cape ... ...ich • Paris • Milan

**ACC. No: 02910798**

**PEARSON EDUCATION LIMITED**

Edinburgh Gate
Harlow CM20 2JE
Tel: +44 (0)1279 623623
Fax: +44 (0)1279 431059
Website: www.pearson.com/uk

First published in Great Britain in 2012

© Heather Morris 2012

The right of Heather Morris to be identified as author of this work has been asserted by her
in accordance with the Copyright, Designs and Patents Act 1988.

Pearson Education is not responsible for the content of third-party internet sites.

ISBN: 978-0-273-76109-9

*British Library Cataloguing-in-Publication Data*
A catalogue record for this book is available from the British Library

*Library of Congress Cataloging-in-Publication Data*
A catalog record for this book is available from the Library of Congress

All rights reserved. No part of this publication may be reproduced, stored in a retrieval
system, or transmitted in any form or by any means, electronic, mechanical, photocopying,
recording or otherwise, without either the prior written permission of the publisher or
a licence permitting restricted copying in the United Kingdom issued by the Copyright
Licensing Agency Ltd, Saffron House, 6–10 Kirby Street, London EC1N 8TS. This book
may not be lent, resold, hired out or otherwise disposed of by way of trade in any form of
binding or cover other than that in which it is published, without the prior consent of the
Publishers.

Microsoft screen shots reprinted with permission from Microsoft Corporation.

10  9  8  7  6  5  4  3  2  1
15  14  13  12  11

Designed by pentacorbig, High Wycombe
Cover image © Michael Hieber – Fotolia.com
Typeset in 11/14 pt ITC Stone Sans by 3
Printed and bound by Scotprint, Haddington.

# Researching your Family History Online

in Simple steps

Heather Morris

# Dedication

For my parents, Robert and Diane Morris

In loving memory of Audrey Morris Marshall

# Acknowledgements

I'm grateful for the help and encouragement I received while writing this book from my husband, my parents and my parents-in-law. I would also like to thank Neil Salkind of the Salkind Literary Agency for his support on this, my first book, and also Joli Ballew for her invaluable feedback on the early chapters.

# Publisher's acknowledgements

*We are grateful to the following for permission to reproduce copyright material:*

Ancestry.co.uk for image on p.3 from 1891 Census collection. Courtesy of The National Archives; www.deadfred.com for photo on p. 23 Photo 14773; FamilySearch website for figures on pp. 2 and 19: blank family tree from www.familysearch.org. FamilySearch; FamilyTreeDNA website www.familytreedna.com/dna-test-kit.aspx for photo on page 158 from DNA testing kit with permission of Family Tree DNA; www.fotosearch.com, (c) Fotosearch.com for image on p.25 from Family coat of arms; The National Archives for images on pp. 3 and 22 from last will and testament sample, figure on p.24 from Ancestry source record sheet, image on p.45 from The National Archives census sheet, all courtesy of The National Archives.

*Screenshots*

1911census.co.uk website for p.51 Search the 1911 census box, p.51 person search results screen, p.52 Choose a payment option box, p.53 secure payment screen, p.133 basic search screen, p.133 street details screen, p.134 Search military records 1656-2005 screen, p.134 Military search results screen; Adobe Systems Inc for p.36 Adobe Reader download screen; Ancestry.co.uk website for p. 48 UK Census Records search by year box, p.48 Searching census records start search box; p.48 Record option boxes screen; p.49 Census/name option box, Subscription fee screen and Search box, p50 Event fields sample box, p.69 Record collections screen and Preview search results screen, p.98 UK incoming passenger list search and search results with save option, p.114 Start 14-day trial screen, p115 Family tree/start a new tree menu and Name your family tree screen, p.116 Burke family tree screen, p.117 Tree settings information page and Pedigree/Family screen, p.118 Subject's birth details screen and Add spouse details screen, p.119 Search records box and Search results box, p120 Birth certificate scan screen and Save this record screen. P121 Ancestry hint screen, p.121 Review record hint screen, p.122 Search all records/military screen, p.123 United Kingdom and Ireland search categories screen and General thread screen, p124 Family group sheet screen, p.179 Forgot your username or password screen, p.181 My account options and p.186 Ancestry image viewer setup box. Barnsley Family History Society for p.167 Barnsley Family History Society homepage. The Barnsley FHS website has been designed and developed by Chantele Smith and Kathryn Brookes; BMDIndex.co.uk website for p.66 BMDIndex.co.uk homepage; The Commonwealth War Graves Commission for p.88 Debt of honour register search, p.89 Casualty details screen both with permission of The Commonwealth War Graves Commission; Convict Records website www.ConvictRecords.com.au for p.110 Convict Records search page; FamilySearch website,www.familysearch.org for p.42 FamilySearch.org search bar, p.107 Index to Bounty Immigrants search results, p.108 Skip passenger lists of New Zealand information screen, p.108 Passenger list search results, p.106 Historical results search results; FamilyTreeDNA website www.familytreedna.com/projects.aspx for p.157 Homepage, p.160 Index project search, p.161 Group project information screen. FreeBMD website, www.freebmd.org.uk for p. 61 FreeBMD Welcome page; pp 8 and 61 FreeBMD search screen, pp 62 and 99 Birth details screen; FreeCEN website www.freecen.org.uk/ for pp 5 and 46 FreeCEN search screen, p.7 Search results box, pp 6 and 47 FreeCEN search results screen; TheGenealogist.co.uk website for p.67 TheGenealogist.co.uk homepage, p.68 Image search BMD Index screen, p.67 percentage box, p.177 The Genealogist Image Viewer screen, © Crown Copyright. Image reproduced by courtesy of the Controller of HMSO and the Office for National Statistics via www. TheGenealogist.co.uk; General Register Office for p.73 certificate types screen and p.75 GRO information, NI Direct website; General Register Office Ireland website for p.55 Homepage; HM Court and Tribunal Service website for p.171 Guide of obtaining copies of probate records screen, © Crown copyright; Library and Archives Canada (LAC) for three webpages in the Passenger List/1865-1922 website pp.104 and 105 Passenger lists search screen, navigation shot and search results © Government of Canada. Reproduced with the permission of the Minister of Public Works and Government Services (Canada (2011) www.collectionscanada.gc.ca; The National Archives for p. 32 The National Archives homepage, p.79 Homepage 2, p.80 sign in screen, p.81 register screen, p.83 DocumentsOnline search screen, p.83 DocumentsOnline Browse Family History: WW1 Campaign Medals screen, p.84 DocumentsOnline family history screen: Royal Marines Register of Service, p.84 DocumentsOnline Image details screenshot, p.85 DocumentsOnline Browse search details, p.85 DocumentsOnline Browse Description screen, p.86 DocumentsOnline Shopping basket screen, p.87 DocumentsOnline email address entry screen, p.87 DocumentsOnline Order confirmation screen, p.90 DocumentsOnline image details screen. p.92 Documents Online Downloading your history screenshot, p.92 DocumentsOnline family history: death duty registers screen, p.93 Nelson, Trafalgar search screen. All courtesy of The National Archives; National Archives of Ireland and the Director of the National Archives of Ireland for p.55 Homepage, p.56 Homepage with search box, p.56 View census images box; News International Syndication (NI Syndication) for p.169 from Times archive Titanic article; Public Record Office Victoria website http://prov.vic.gov.au for p.109 Index to Assisted British Immigration search screen and search details results box, reproduced with the permission of the Keeper of Public Records, Public Record Office Victoria, Australia; RRS Discovery website http://www.rrsdiscovery.com for p.38 Opening genealogy fact sheet box; Society of Genealogists website for p.168 Society of Genealogists homepage.; University of Portsmouth. for p.172 A vision of Britain through time homepage. "Great Britain Historical GIS Project (2011) 'A Vision of Britain through Time'. University of Portsmouth, www.visionofbritain.org.uk "; West Yorkshire Archive Service for p.165 Homepage from West Yorkshire Joint Service website; Yahoo! Inc for p.183 Step 2 message delivery; Yahoo UK for pp. 31 and 33 Yahoo tool bar screenshot, p.34 Yahoo! UK search results – Geneaology Scotland, p.35 Yahoo! UK search results – Geneaology Channel Islands, p.39 Yahoo! UK toolbar with Bookmarks menu pulled down, p.39 Yahoo! UK bookmarked page, p.40 Yahoo! Inc History pull-down list. p.144 Yahoo! UK & Ireland Groups Sign in screenshot. Reproduced with permission of Yahoo! Inc. ©2011 Yahoo! Inc. YAHOO! and the YAHOO! logo are registered trademarks of Yahoo! Inc.

In some instances we have been unable to trace the owners of copyright material, and we would appreciate any information that would enable us to do so.

# Contents at a glance

# Use your computer with confidence

Get to grips with practical computing tasks with minimal time, fuss and bother.

*In Simple Steps guides* guarantee immediate results. They tell you everything you need to know on a specific application; from the most essential tasks to master, to every activity you'll want to accomplish, through to solving the most common problems you'll encounter.

## Helpful features

To build your confidence and help you to get the most out of your online research, practical hints, tips and shortcuts feature on every page:

 **ALERT:** Explains and provides practical solutions to the most commonly encountered problems

 **HOT TIP:** Time and effort saving shortcuts

 **SEE ALSO:** Points you to other related tasks and information

 **DID YOU KNOW?** Additional features to explore

**WHAT DOES THIS MEAN?**
Jargon and technical terms explained in plain English

# Practical. Simple. Fast.

# Contents

## Top 10 Online Research Tips

## 1 Review genealogy basics

## 2 Get started on the internet

## 3 Search census data

## 4 Find birth, marriage and death information

## 5 Explore the National Archives

## 6 Trace family migrants

## 9 Connect with others online

## 10 Use DNA testing to support your research

## 11 Continue your search with other sources

## Top 10 Online Research Problems Solved

# Top 10 Online Research Tips

# Tip 1: Gather your family records and start a tree

You may be surprised at how much you already know about your family history and how much information you have hidden away in files and cupboards. Spend time now, at the beginning of your research, to think through the details of your family and find records that will help with your ongoing research.

**1** Write down what you know about your family members.

**2** Locate any documents relating to the people on your list.

**3** Update your initial family tree with the information you have gathered from your first search through family records.

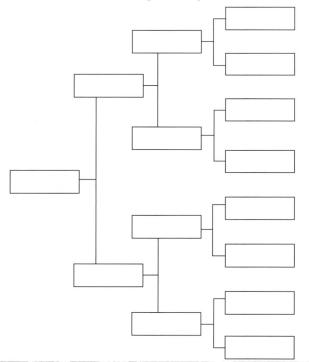

 **HOT TIP:** Drawing a simple family tree can help you visualise where there are gaps in your knowledge.

 **HOT TIP:** Focus on information such as their full names and approximate birth or death dates. Include the place of birth, marriage or death if you know it.

**?** **DID YOU KNOW?**
Family bibles can be used as a primary source if the details were written near the time of the event.

# Tip 2: Understand URLs

A Uniform Resource Locator (URL) is a unique address for a website. Like a telephone number, each one is different and is associated with a specific location (site) on the internet. Unlike phone numbers, they are easy to remember as they mostly consist of the words you associate with the site. For example, the URL for the National Archives is www.thenationalarchives.gov.uk. Find this URL by following the directions below.

**1** Open your web browser.

**2** Move your cursor to the end of the existing URL in the address bar and click the address bar.

**! ALERT:** A URL is not the same as an email address.

**3** Type in the URL (www.nationalarchives.gov.uk) and the highlighted text will automatically disappear.

**4** Click Enter.

**? DID YOU KNOW?**
The last part or suffix of the URL identifies the type of address. In this case, the National Archives is a government website (.gov), located in the UK (.uk). Other suffixes are .co = company, .ac = school or university, .org = organisation.

## WHAT DOES THIS MEAN?

**http://**: is short for hypertext transfer protocol. In a nutshell, it is the way information is exchanged between one computer and another and is part of many URLs. It isn't necessary to type http:// each time you type the URL.

# Tip 3: Create safe user names and passwords

As you begin to frequent the popular genealogy websites, you will be asked to create an account to use these sites. In order to create an account, you will need a user name and a password. A safe user name will consist of part of your name and some combination of numbers. Use the following tips to create a safe user name and password:

- Avoid using your full name to protect your identity. Instead, use part of your name or even an alias that will be easy for you to remember.
- Avoid using your birth date as part of the number combination.
- Don't use your email address as a user name.
- Don't use your email password as the password for your website account.
- Write down your password in a safe place away from your computer.
- Consider using a symbol in your password combination (i.e. Dav02*).

Sign In

User Name

Password

Sign In

Forgot your user name or password?

FamilySearch.org — Free Family History and Genealogy Records - Mozilla Firefox

File   Edit   View   History   Bookmarks   Yahoo!   Tools   Help

familysearch.org   https://www.familysearch.org/

 **HOT TIP:** A locked padlock symbol on your web browser's address bar also shows you are on a secure site.

**! ALERT:** Make purchases online only when using a trusted website.

## WHAT DOES THIS MEAN?

**S:** you will see an additional s in the URLs of some websites (https:). The s stands for secure and is there to show you are on a secure site.

# Tip 4: Search the census records at FreeCEN

This website is run entirely by volunteers with the goal of making genealogical data available to family researchers for free. They have transcribed many census records from 1841 to 1891. Some of these records have been fully transcribed and contain all of the information from the original census, including residence, occupation and details of household members.

**1** Go to www.freecen.org.uk.

**2** Click Search the Database.

**3** Click the Year menu and select a census year to search.

**4** Enter the details for your relative, select a county or census place and click Find.

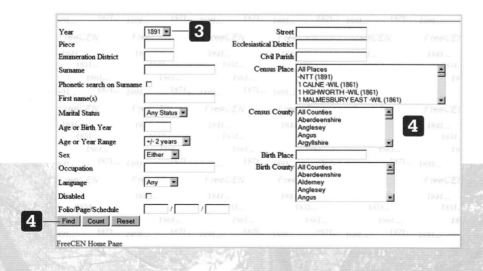

**UK Census Online**

*"Bringing YOUR ancestors to YOU, free of charge!"*

Have YOU ever thought of the benefit of the U.K. Census data being centrally av

This project aims to provide a "free-to-view" online searchable database of the 19th century

**FreeCEN** is part of **FreeUKGEN**, an initiative aimed at helping make high quality primary (or search, information retrieval system.
Other projects associated with the FreeUKGEN initiative are **FreeBMD** and **FreeREG**.

**Volunteers**

Many volunteers world-wide are working on the transcription.

The number of volunteers has grown since its inception in 1999 to 125 in December 2000. It

We are constantly looking for new volunteers. We need help with Transcribing and Checkir volunteer to help with. To contact the Coordinator for a County that you are interested in he

As well as the 1891 Census we are also working on the 1841, 1851, 1861 and 1871 census. W page on **http://www.freecen.org.uk/statistics.html**

Please remember to keep coming back to check as we add more Census DATA.

**Search the Database**    Informatio    ut Coverage

Database last updated    **Database Coverage**
Friday, 18-Mar-2011 23:10:02 GMT    **Recent Additions**

On Mon 4 Apr 2011 FreeCEN users did
31,058 searches. (**Details**)

| Year | 1891 | | Street | |
| Piece | | | Ecclesiastical District | |
| Emmeration District | | | Civil Parish | |
| Surname | | | Census Place | All Places / -NTT (1891) / 1 CALNE -WIL (1861) / 1 HIGHWORTH -WIL (1861) / 1 MALMESBURY EAST -WIL (1861) |
| Phonetic search on Surname | □ | | | |
| First name(s) | | | | |
| Marital Status | Any Status | | Census County | All Counties / Aberdeenshire / Anglesey / Angus / Argyllshire |
| Age or Birth Year | | | | |
| Age or Year Range | +/- 2 years | | | |
| Sex | Either | | Birth Place | |
| Occupation | | | Birth County | All Counties / Aberdeenshire / Alderney / Anglesey / Angus |
| Language | Any | | | |
| Disabled | □ | | | |
| Folio/Page/Schedule | / / | | | |

Find    Count    Reset

FreeCEN Home Page

**5** Review the results for your family member and click Show Household to view the census information.

**6** Record the information into your family tree and make a note of the census record details.

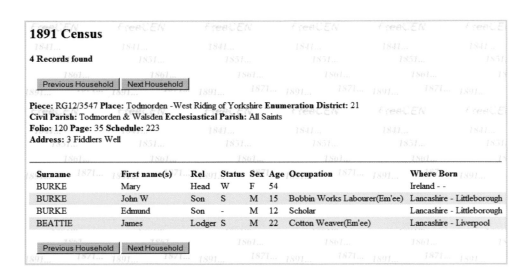

**1891 Census**

**4 Records found**

Previous Household | Next Household

**Piece:** RG12/3547 **Place:** Todmorden -West Riding of Yorkshire **Enumeration District:** 21
**Civil Parish:** Todmorden & Walsden **Ecclesiastical Parish:** All Saints
**Folio:** 120 **Page:** 35 **Schedule:** 223
**Address:** 3 Fiddlers Well

| Surname | First name(s) | Rel | Status | Sex | Age | Occupation | Where Born |
|---------|---------------|-----|--------|-----|-----|------------|------------|
| BURKE | Mary | Head | W | F | 54 | | Ireland - - |
| BURKE | John W | Son | S | M | 15 | Bobbin Works Labourer(Em'ee) | Lancashire - Littleborough |
| BURKE | Edmund | Son | - | M | 12 | Scholar | Lancashire - Littleborough |
| BEATTIE | James | Lodger | S | M | 22 | Cotton Weaver(Em'ee) | Lancashire - Liverpool |

Previous Household | Next Household

**HOT TIP:** Save time by looking first at the statistics section of the website to see which censuses have been transcribed and added to the site.

**SEE ALSO:** Don't be discouraged if you can't find your relatives on this index – there are many other sources of census data online.

**ALERT:** Keep this website bookmarked and check back often as they are constantly adding new census information to the site.

**SEE ALSO:** ww1.scotlandspeople. gov.uk: this website contains more complete records of censuses from Scotland (for a fee).

# Tip 5: Search for records on FreeBMD

This website is run by the same volunteers who run the FreeCEN site. It has more than 200 million records transcribed and linked to the site, with an excellent number of records for the years 1837–1929. This should be your first stop when looking for free BMD information on the web. The database is updated every month.

**1** Go to www.freebmd.org.uk and click Search.

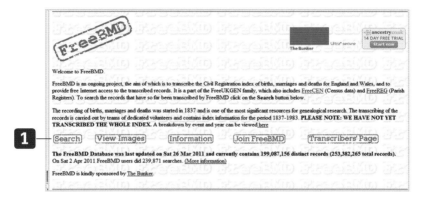

**SEE ALSO:** A more complete set of BMD records and parish data for Scotland is available at www.scotlandspeople.gov.uk. The site charges a fee to view records but it is an excellent source of family history data for anyone with roots in Scotland.

**2** Select the type of records you are looking for (i.e. all births, marriages, deaths).

**3** Enter the details for your relative and select district if you know it.

**4** Select a county to search.

**5** Choose a date range that covers at least two years.

**6** Click Find.

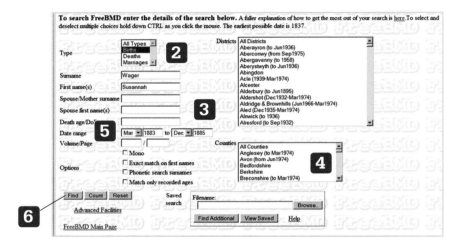

**7** Click Revise Query if you don't find a record you were looking for.

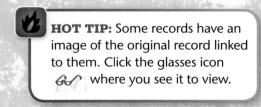

**HOT TIP:** Some records have an image of the original record linked to them. Click the glasses icon where you see it to view.

**ALERT:** Write down the full citation, including district, volume and page.

**ALERT:** You must select a county or the search will not function.

# Tip 6: Search emigration records on ancestorsonboard

This site is a great source of information about your relative who left the UK for another country. There is a searchable database of passenger lists records from 1890 to 1960 for people who left for locations including the US, Australia, Canada, New Zealand and South Africa. If you registered and bought credits on the 1911census site or the findmypast site, you can use your credits to search here.

**1** Go to www.ancestorsonboard.com.

**2** Enter the details for your relative.

**3** Select a destination country and port if you know it and click Search.

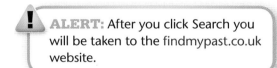

**ALERT:** After you click Search you will be taken to the findmypast.co.uk website.

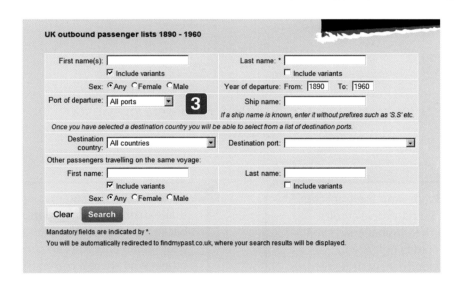

**4** Click View transcript.

## passenger transcript details

| | | |
|---|---|---|
| Name: | **Mrs WALKER** | |
| Date of departure: | **28 April 1922** | |
| Port of departure: | **Southampton** | |
| Passenger destination port: | **Cape, South Africa** | |
| Passenger destination: | **Cape, South Africa** | |
| Date of Birth: | **1895 (calculated from age)** | |
| Age: | **27** | |
| Marital status: | **Married** | |
| Sex: | **Female** | |
| Occupation: | | |
| Passenger recorded on: | **Page 2 of 8** | |

PRINTER FRIENDLY VERSION

VIEW ORIGINAL IMAGE

The following people with the same last name travelled on this voyage: -

| | | |
|---|---|---|
| **Mr N L WALKER** | Page 2 of 8 | View transcript |
| **Mr R Mcneill WALKER** | Page 5 of 8 | View transcript |

**4**

| | |
|---|---|
| Ship: | **ARMADALE CASTLE** |
| Official Number: | **118350** |
| Master's name: | **H Strong** |
| Steamship Line: | **Union-Castle Mail Steamship Coy Ltd** |
| Where bound: | **South Africa** |
| Square feet: | **6670** |
| Registered tonnage: | **12973** |
| Passengers on voyage: | **199** |

REPORT TRANSCRIPTION CHANGE

**ALERT:** Viewing the transcript will cost you only five credits. Viewing the original image will cost 30 credits unless you have a subscription to view these records.

**SEE ALSO:** Joining message boards that explore a specific country or ethnic background can provide useful clues for your search and you can connect with others who share a common heritage. See Chapter 9 for information on how to do this.

**SEE ALSO:** There are also some records on the site for individuals who left for different parts of Asia, South America, the Caribbean and West Africa.

**HOT TIP:** The passenger lists on this site include not only emigrants but also individuals who left for business or tourism.

# Tip 7: Consider joining ancestry.co.uk

The easy-to-navigate site, wealth of records and family tree tool have made Ancestry the most popular genealogy site worldwide. The website below is dedicated to UK family history (as opposed to ancestry.com) and all of the records and resources are designed to meet the needs of researchers in the UK. With an ancestry subscription you can do the following:

- Sign up for a 14 day-free trial.
- Attach documents from the site to your online family tree.
- Search the large collection of military and immigration records.
- Browse the criminal registers, probate records and wills.
- Upgrade to a worldwide membership.

**ALERT:** Worldwide membership gives you access to Australian and US immigration records as well as a variety of Irish historical records.

 **HOT TIP:** The free trial is based on the type of subscription you are interested in.

 **ALERT:** If you continue to use pay-as-you-go credits, they must be used within 14 days or you will lose them.

# Tip 8: Consider joining findmypast.co.uk

This website is dedicated exclusively to researching family history in the UK. Presently, it is the only genealogy site to have the 1911 census records and it has many other unique features that are worth considering. With findmypast.co.uk you can:

- Buy credits that can be used for up to a year.
- Choose a 6- or 12-month subscription.
- Search for emigrants who left the UK.
- Search census records by address as well as name.
- Match marriage registry information for both spouses.
- Explore overseas and military records.

**ALERT:** The 14-day trial will provide you with a foundation membership for 14 days, which allows you to search BMDs and census records but not specialist records.

**SEE ALSO:** If you had relatives in London from the 16th to the 18th century, you can search for them in the fascinating Boyd's Inhabitants of London and Boyd's Family Units on this site.

# Tip 9: Find a mailing list on Rootsweb

Rootsweb was one of the earliest family history communities online. It boasts more than 30,000 international mailing lists and has countless members active online. The community is now hosted by Ancestry.com but you can join most of its mailing lists for free. However, some groups restrict access to members of a specific group, such as local history societies or surname groups.

**1** Go to http://lists.rootsweb.ancestry.com.

**2** Enter a term into the Find a mailing list field and click Find.

**3** Read the group's description or click more to check whether the group is of interest to you.

**4** Follow the instructions to register.

**5** Or note the subscription address and launch your mail program.

**6** Enter the address in your email, type *subscribe* in the subject line and send.

## Find a List Search

Viewing **1-25** of **501** matches from **32,097** mailing lists        1 2 3 4 5 6 7 8 9 10 11 12 13 14 15 16 17 18 19 20 21 | Next

| List Name | Description | | Location | Surname | Category |
|---|---|---|---|---|---|
| LONDON | London | | England, London / Greater London | | |
| ADAMS-ENG-LONDON | The ADAMS-ENG-LONDON mailing list is for the discussion and... more | | | ADAMS | |
| LONDON-LIFE | A mailing list for the discussion and sharing... more | | England | | |
| EOLFHS-MEMBERS | A mailing list for the members of the East of London... more | | England, London / Greater London | | Genealogical Societies |
| 1-25TH-LONDON | The 1-25th London Cycle Regiment in WWI. Used... more | | England | | Military: UK |
| LONDON-SURNAME | Discussing and sharing of information regarding... more | | | LONDON | |
| FOSTER-RICHARD | The FOSTER-RICHARD mailing list is for the discussion... more | | | FOSTER | |
| REDFIELD | primarily on surname REDFIELD, but also to include... more | | | REDFIELD | |
| CTNEWLON | New London County, CT | | USA, Connecticut, New London | | |
| TOLPUDDLE | The TOLPUDDLE mailing list is for the discussion... more | | | TOLPUDDLE | |
| LONDON-COMPANYS | A mailing list for anyone with an interest in the... more | | | | Occupations |
| ENGLAND-ROOTS | A mailing list for anyone with a genealogical interest... more | | England | | |
| FOSTER-ENGLAND | Foster surname and variations in England. | | | FOSTER | |
| ROGERS-JAMES-CT | This mailing list will be of interest to the descendants... more | | | ROGERS | |
| GUYFAWKES | | | England | | |
| OXFORDSHIRE | Oxfordshire | | England, Oxfordshire / Oxon | | |
| Middlesex_County_UK | Middlesex County | | England, Middlesex | | |
| DEVON | Devonshire | | England, Devon or Devonshire | | |
| NORTHANTS | Northampton | | England, Northampton | | |

**! ALERT:** If you click the link to subscribe, it will work only if you are on your own computer. If the link does not work for some other reason, you will need to follow steps 5 and 6.

**🔥 HOT TIP:** You can often browse the archives of the groups prior to joining. You can also get a sense of how busy the group is by looking at how many emails are sent each month.

# Tip 10: Join a local history society

Some of the best information for your area of research can be found in a local history society. Enthusiasm for local and family history has grown in recent years and many counties, towns and even villages have formed societies to meet the surge in interest. Many societies use mailing lists or forums to keep members up to date.

The benefits of joining a local society include:

- Learn about the records available for the area and how to access them.
- Attend regular meetings and presentations.
- Meet others researching a shared surname.
- Receive newsletters with member updates and research tips.

**SEE ALSO:** Scottish Family History societies www.safhs.org.uk.

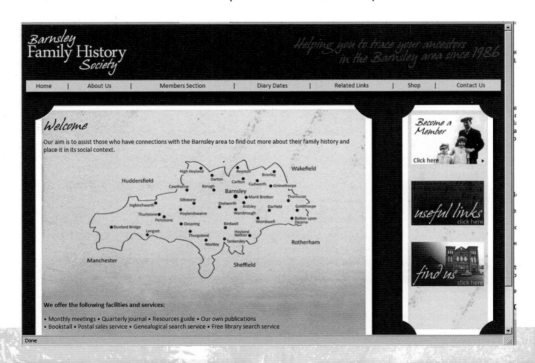

**SEE ALSO:** Search the list of societies on the Federation of Family Historian Societies website www.ffhs.org.uk/members2/alpha.php for a society near you.

**ALERT:** Most societies will charge a modest annual membership fee.

# 1 Review genealogy basics

# Introduction

The internet has dramatically changed the way family historians conduct their research and make discoveries about their ancestors. What previously might have taken months of travelling to archives, history centres and libraries can now be accomplished at home on your computer. You can also connect with other genealogists, meet distant relatives and trade research with others on a shared family line.

# Understand primary sources

The foundation of all good family history research is the primary source. A primary source is a record that was created near the time an event occurred. It may be a document such as a birth, marriage or death certificate (BMD). You need a primary source to help establish the facts of your family history.

Other primary sources to support your research, some of which can be found online, include the following:

- Census records – information about the population of England and Wales, recorded every ten years since 1801 (except 1941).

**DID YOU KNOW?**
Newspapers, published family histories and local histories are considered secondary sources – evidence that was recorded well after an event took place. Use these sources to help guide your research, but don't use them as evidence that something took place.

**ALERT:** Census records for Ireland began in 1821 and for Scotland in 1841.

- BMD registers – since 1837, the law has required births, marriages and deaths in England and Wales to be registered with the register office where the event took place.
- Parish registers – prior to 1837, information about baptisms, marriages and burial records can be found in the parish registers where your ancestor lived.
- Military service papers – look for information about regiment, division, name of ship and rank, in addition to the person's name and approximate dates of service.

**ALERT:** While registration of BMDs began in 1837 in the UK, not everyone participated in registering their family's details. Unfortunately, your ancestors may be among them.

# Gather your family records and start a tree

You may be surprised at how much you already know about your family history and how much information you have hidden away in files and cupboards. Spend time now, at the beginning of your research, thinking through the details of your family and find records that will help with your ongoing research.

**1** Write down what you know about your family members.

**2** Locate any documents relating to the people on your list.

**3** Update your initial family tree with the information you have gathered from your first search through family records.

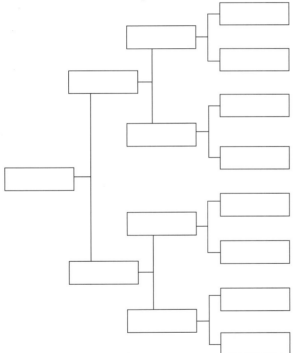

 **HOT TIP:** Drawing a simple family tree can help you visualise where there are gaps in your knowledge.

 **HOT TIP:** Focus on information such as their full names and approximate birth or death dates.

 **HOT TIP:** Include the place of birth, marriage or death if you know it.

 **DID YOU KNOW?** Family bibles can also be used as a primary source if the details were written near the time of the event.

# Buy copies of birth, marriage and death certificates

The information contained on birth, marriage and death certificates is invaluable to the family historian. They provide you with historical proof of the life events, family relationships, residences and occupations of your ancestors. These records also contain important clues about other family members and can serve as a starting point for further research.

- Gather the basic information about the ancestor you want a certificate for (first name, approximate birth year, surname).
- Purchase BMD certificates at the local registry office where the event took place.
- Purchase BMD certificates through the General Register Office (GRO) by phone, email or online.

**ALERT:** Buy certificates only through the GRO or at the local registry office. Some genealogy websites add a substantial fee for a certificate that should cost about £10.

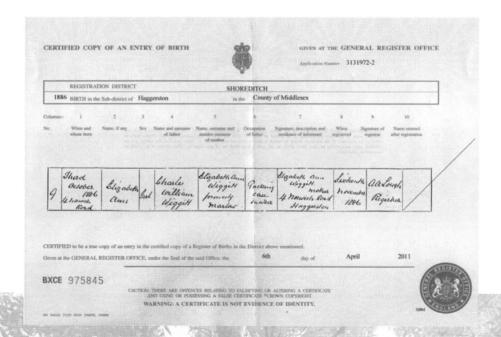

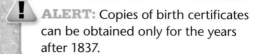

**HOT TIP:** Buy certificates only for the family line you are most interested in researching.

**ALERT:** Copies of birth certificates can be obtained only for the years after 1837.

# Talk to relatives

Talking to aunts, grandparents and distant cousins may provide you with information about your family you didn't know to ask about. While you will be looking for facts and information, take time to listen and find out what your relatives were like. Hearing these stories from older relatives is one of the real joys of genealogy.

**1** Check with relatives to see whether they can add to your preliminary family tree.

**2** Bring your family tree and any photos or other family documents that you found in your initial search.

**3** Listen as much as you talk, but also try to get help with the gaps in your knowledge.

**4** Ask for more details about any family tales you may have heard.

Questions to ask aunt Sarah

What was he like?

Did he have a nickname?

Was he in the military?

Can you tell me about...?

 **HOT TIP:** Consider tape recording your interview if your family member doesn't object.

 **HOT TIP:** After you've completed the interview, be sure to ask whether your relative has any original documents or photographs which they might allow you to view or copy.

# Uncover other sources of your family history

Many of these additional sources, particularly letters and diaries, will add meaningful insights into the lives of your ancestors. You may not be able to locate all of these items during your initial search, but keep your eyes out for them as you continue your research and talk to relatives.

- Wills – there are good records of family wills in many English counties, dating back to the Middle Ages.

- Gravestone inscriptions – include information about birth and death dates but also something of family relationships.

- Books – look for personal inscriptions in the front of the book.

- Maps – can be of family land or a historic map of the village or town where your ancestor resided.

- Newspaper clippings or obituaries – look for the names of extended family members.

- Diaries and letters – look for specific information about family, but also use them just to get a sense of the time and what the person was like.

**HOT TIP:** Wills can be vital to family history because most contain information about the author's extended family, their residence and occupation.

**HOT TIP:** A person's collection of books can tell you a good deal about that person's interests and maybe a little something of what they were like.

**ALERT:** Keep older original documents in acid-free boxes to help preserve them.

# Use family photographs

Old photographs can be some of the most meaningful artefacts in your family archives (or cupboards). They have the potential to provide information about family relationships, social standing or military service. They also give you a sense of what living at a certain time period may have been like.

1. Look at all of the photos you have, even if you don't recognise everyone in the photo.

2. Look on the back of the photos for names and dates.

3. Examine for the following clues if no information is available, including:

   - How many children are in the photo.
   - Age differences between the husband and wife.
   - Style of dress (to date the photo).

 **HOT TIP:** Show your pictures of mystery ancestors to relatives at family gatherings to get help in identifying them.

**ALERT:** Store your photographs carefully as they are prone to mould and can be destroyed by direct sunlight. Look for cardboard boxes made from acid-free material or plastic covers free of PVC.

**? DID YOU KNOW?**
You can take your ageing photographs to a photo restoration service. Some services will also digitise the image for you, which you can use in your online work later.

# Learn good research practices

Making new discoveries about your ancestors is exciting, but you should also try to approach the task with some discipline. You want a family history that is accurate, well documented and that you will be proud to share with others. Here are a few general rules to keep in mind:

- Start with your own family and work backwards.
- Stick to one family line at a time.
- Check others' work.
- Document your sources.

| Person | Description of source and citation | Location | Date of search | Notes |
|---|---|---|---|---|
| William A Taylor | 1891 Census collection Civil parish: Whitechapel St. Mary (London) ED: 7 | ancestry.co.uk | 4/8/11 | No record of siblings in this census. Check 1901 census. |
| William A Taylor | Birth Registar 1886 Quarter: Oct-Dec. District: Shoreditch (London) Volume: 1c Page: 125 | ancestry.co.uk | 7/8/11 | |

- Maintain a healthy scepticism of any source, even official ones.
- Cross check details for an individual in more than one primary source.
- Keep clear records.

 **HOT TIP:** Plan your research. Have a specific goal in mind and keep the plan in front of you when you begin your research.

**ALERT:** Check that the information you have makes sense. A person born in 1946 is unlikely to have been the mother of someone born in 1956, no matter that they share the same parish.

 **HOT TIP:** Connect with a local genealogical group or family history society early in your research.

# Understand the history of surnames

The history of surnames is a source of both fascination and frustration for family historians. While there is good evidence of the existence of surnames since the Middle Ages, they have by no means been fixed since that time. However, you can garner valuable clues about your family's ancestors by simply learning something about their names. Most surnames are based on the following sources:

- Father's name – Williamson for the son of William. There are other well-known equivalents in Welsh, Scottish and Irish families (-ap for son in Wales, and O- or Mc- in Scotland and Ireland.)
- Location – an individual with the last name of Durham most likely had an ancestor who was born or lived there for a long time. There are natural equivalents as well, such as Meadows and Woods.
- Occupation – a Cooper made barrels; Sawyer (one who saws) was a carpenter, etc.
- Nicknames – a Longfellow may well have had an ancestor who was tall in stature. This type of origin is less likely than those above.

▶ **SEE ALSO:** Explore the history and geographic distribution of your surname at http://gbnames.publicprofiler.org.

▶ **SEE ALSO:** There are online research groups devoted to unique family surnames. See Chapter 9 for more information on how to find and join a group related to one of your family surnames.

# Try alternative spellings in your search

Whether due to a simple error in the records or a deliberate attempt by your ancestor to change their identity or social position, many family names have been substantially altered since their creation. Sometimes your ancestor may have used different spellings at different times in their lives.

**1** List every possible variation of the surname you can think of.

**2** Keep in mind the following when considering alternative spellings:

- Double consonant in the middle of the name.
- Silent e at the end of the name.
- Difference between how names are spelled and pronounced (e.g. Dalziel).

**3** Use a telephone directory to look for alternative spellings (e.g. Wigitt, Wiggitt, Wiggett).

**ALERT:** Check that all of the primary record details (birth, marriage, death) and family relationships correspond to the person you are thinking of when you search under an alternative name spelling.

```
Wigg A.M, 59 Hollydown Wy E11 .........................01-556 5677
Wigg E.W, 111 Gloucester Rd E17 .....................01-531 6144
Wigg F.W, 24 Farmer Rd E10..............................01-539 2405
Wigg J.F, 22 Hawthorn Gro,Enfield ....................01-363 6805
Wigg R.D, 111 Princes Rd,Buckhurst Hl...............01-504 6257
Wigg R.E, 28 Alpha Rd E4 ..................................01-529 5095
Wigg R.J, 25 Beechwood Dv,Woodford Gn...........01-504 9589
Wigg R.K, 17 Oxford Rd,Enfield...........................01-805 0916
Wigg Stephan C.J, 9 Napier Rd,Enfield................01-805 8601
Wigg T, 79 Coppermill La E17 ............................01-521 5889
Wiggan I, 116 Edward Rd E17.............................01-520 4959
Wiggan Stanley, 123 Rogate Ho,Muir Rd E5..........01-985 4980
Wigger A.W, 17 Shortlands Rd E10......................01-556 3308
Wiggett D.C, 34 Shelley Ho,Shakespeare Wlk N16...01-254 9568
Wiggett J, 94 Trumpington Rd E7 .......................01-534 1116
Wiggett M,
        118 George Downing Est,Cazenove Rd N16...01-806 2143
Wiggett Roy, 30 Smalley Clo N16.........................01-249 1294
```

 **HOT TIP:** Make sure you pursue the surnames of your female ancestors as well as the males.

 **HOT TIP:** Apply the same rules when you are having difficulty with the place names (villages, towns) of your relatives.

# Get organised

It is important to organise your information so that you can easily access and use it when you need to. Most family historians will stop and start their work many times. Having a simple system of organisation helps to keep track of the research you have completed and the research that needs to be done.

- Group your research by surname.
- File additional documents by government records, BMDs, personal family papers and photographs.
- Use consistent labels for your records, particularly vital information such as births, marriages and deaths. Consider these:

  Birth – b.

  Marriage – m.

  Died – d.

  Place born – p.

  Occupation – occ.

- Make note of missing documents and records you need to locate in a To Do section of your files.
- Keep a record of completed work.

**Family Group Sheet**

| Husband | | Occupation: | | | notes |
|---|---|---|---|---|---|
| | Date | City | County | Parish | |
| born | | | | | |
| Christened | | | | | |
| married | | | | | |
| died | | | | | |
| buried | | | | | |
| Father | | | | | |
| Mother | | | | | |
| **Wife** | | **Occupation:** | | | notes |
| | Date | City | County | Parish | |
| born | | | | | |
| Christened | | | | | |
| died | | | | | |
| buried | | | | | |
| Father | | | | | |
| Mother | | | | | |

| Children | Birth d-m-y | Birthplace | Date/place marriage | Death date | notes |
|---|---|---|---|---|---|
| 1 | | | | | |
| 2 | | | | | |
| 3 | | | | | |
| 4 | | | | | |
| 5 | | | | | |
| 6 | | | | | |
| 7 | | | | | |
| 8 | | | | | |
| 9 | | | | | |
| 10 | | | | | |

 **HOT TIP:** Choose a method that works for you and stick with it.

 **HOT TIP:** Remember to spell out middle names and to keep track of female ancestors by their maiden name.

 **SEE ALSO:** Once you are online, search for free genealogy forms, including pedigree charts, family group sheets and research logs. These will help you organise your work.

# 2 Get started on the internet

# Introduction

The internet is a powerful tool for research, learning and connecting with others. You may get lost the first few times you surf and spend hours finding your way around. In this chapter we will review the basics of internet searches, file types and how to download files to your computer. At the end you will be able to navigate the major family history sites with ease.

It's important to note that websites change all the time. They get updated, and page elements are often relocated to different parts of the page or removed altogether. What you'll find here and throughout this book is what was available when this book went to press; what you see when you actually start your search may differ.

# Understand URLs

A Uniform Resource Locator (URL) is a unique address for a website. Like a telephone number, each one is different and is associated with a specific location (site) on the internet. Unlike phone numbers, they are easy to remember as they mostly consist of the words you associate with the site. For example, the URL for the National Archives is www.thenationalarchives.gov.uk. Find this URL by following the directions below.

1 Open your web browser.

2 Move your cursor to the end of the existing URL in the address bar and click the address bar.

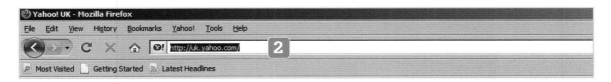

---

**? DID YOU KNOW?**

The last part or suffix of the URL identifies the type of address. In this case, the National Archives is a government website (.gov), located in the UK (.uk). Other suffixes include .co = company, .ac = school or university, .org = organisation.

**! ALERT:** A URL is not the same as an email address.

3 Type in the URL (www.nationalarchives.gov.uk) and the highlighted text will automatically disappear.

4 Click Enter.

## WHAT DOES THIS MEAN?

**http://**: is short for hypertext transfer protocol. In a nutshell, it is the way information is exchanged between one computer and another and is part of many URLs. It isn't necessary to type http:// each time you type the URL.

# Search using key words

In addition to typing the URL of a website into your address bar, you can perform broader searches on search engines by using key words. Search engines, such as Yahoo! and Google, sort through millions of Internet sites and present you with the most relevant results based on your key words.

1 Type uk.search.yahoo.com into your address bar and press Return.

2 Type Genealogy Scotland into the search box and press Search.

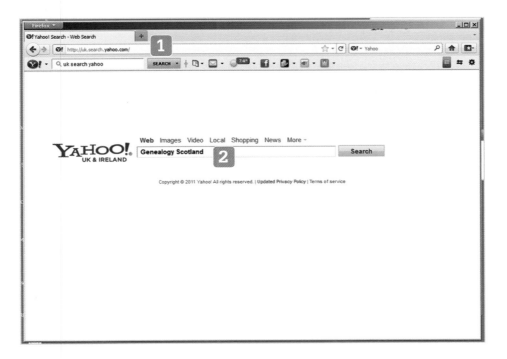

**! ALERT:** There are millions of genealogy websites on the internet, not all of them worth your time. Use the websites from this book and those that are associated with either an academic or government institution (ending in ac.uk or gov.uk).

**3** Click on a link that interests you.

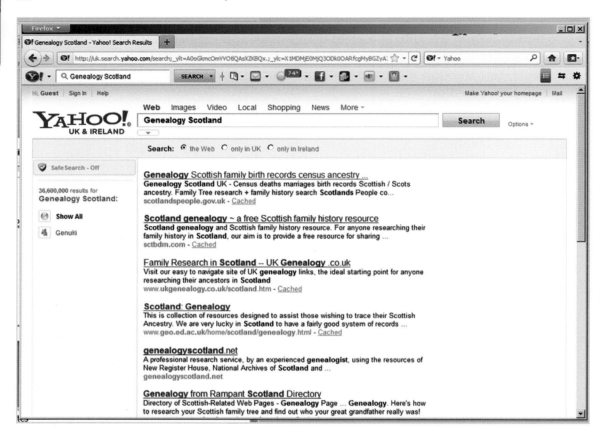

**? DID YOU KNOW?**

Websites consist of many different pages and navigating around them can be confusing. Most websites have a Home button. You can click on Home and that will take you to the first page you arrived at when you typed in the URL.

# Know which key words produce results

One problem with conducting internet searches is the large volume of results you will get. There are a few ways to narrow your search to produce results that are helpful to you. Use the following tips:

- Search with phrases only.
- Avoid pronouns (me, our, his), articles (a, the) and conjunctions (and, but).
- Use quotation marks around the search term. Searching this way limits the search to the exact phrase entered.
- Use alternative search words if your initial key words do not produce results.

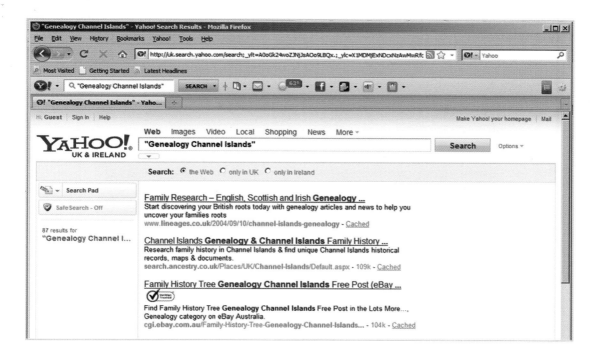

 **SEE ALSO:** Most search engines have a feature called 'predictive text'. When you begin typing your query, a box appears below with suggested key words. You can move your cursor to one of the suggestions and click on one that interests you.

**HOT TIP:** Use the Back button when you want to go back to a page you were viewing previously.

# Get Adobe Reader

You will find many files that you'll want to keep during your internet research. One of the most common file types is the PDF (Portable Document Format). The PDF is a file type created by Adobe that can be downloaded, opened and read on all types of computers. You need to download the Reader before you can open or save these documents to your computer.

**1** Go to http://get.adobe.com/reader.

**2** Click Download now.

**3** Click Install now when the software installation box appears.

**4** Restart your web browser (you will be prompted to do this).

**5** If your browser prevents you from downloading the Reader using the steps above, do the following:

- Click Allow in the upper right corner of your browser.
- Follow steps 3 and 4 above.

**? DID YOU KNOW?**

PDF files are more than just text files. They can contain images relevant to the family historian, such as wills and maps.

**? DID YOU KNOW?**

Many PDF files may read like Word documents but cannot be typed into or altered like a Word document. If you want to make notes on a PDF, you can print it out and write them in by hand.

# Open a PDF file

Now that you have Adobe Acrobat reader installed, you can open and save PDF files quickly.

**1** Go to www.nationalarchives.gov.uk.

**2** Click Records.

**3** Click In-depth research guides.

**4** Click a file from the alphabetical list that you want to open.

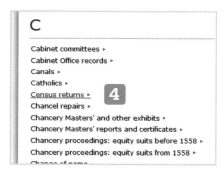

**5** Click Download as a PDF. A new window will open and you can view the document.

**6** You can either close the window when you have finished reading or save the PDF to your computer (click Save in the upper left corner of the window).

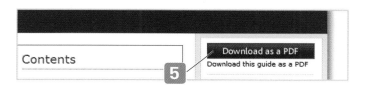

---

**? DID YOU KNOW?**
Most of the content available for download at the National Archives website is in PDFs.

**▶ SEE ALSO:** The National Archives online – spend some time browsing through other research guides for great information on the site's resources.

# Download other file types

Occasionally you will come across types of files on the internet that are not PDFs. Common file types include .xls (Microsoft Excel), .doc (Microsoft Word), .jpg (a generic picture file). You'll see others, too. You'll need to download these files and save them to your computer.

**1** Click the link provided for the document.

**2** If prompted to save the document:
   a. Click Save.
   b. Browse on your computer to the location where you'd like to save the document.
   c. Name the document appropriately.
   d. Click Save.

**3** If prompted to open the document:
   a. Click OK when the dialogue box appears.
   b. Click File and Save as (or choose another option as appropriate).
   c. Choose a place on your computer you will remember.
   d. Name the file appropriately.
   e. Click Save.

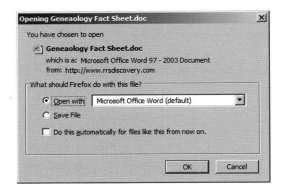

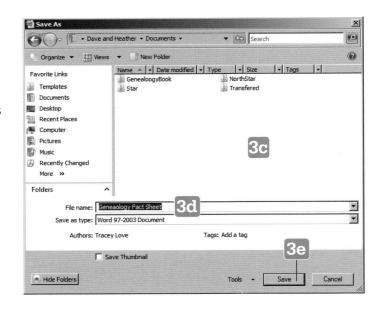

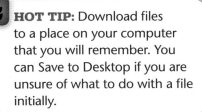

**HOT TIP:** Download files to a place on your computer that you will remember. You can Save to Desktop if you are unsure of what to do with a file initially.

**ALERT:** Click Yes if prompted by your computer to scan a file before downloading. This is one way the software on your computer keeps you safe from viruses and other common problems.

# Configure a bookmark or favourite

After spending some time on the internet, you will find websites on your own that you will want to return to. Rather than write down the URL of every site, you can save the information in your browser and locate your favourite sites with just a click.

**1** Click Bookmarks, then click Bookmark This Page.

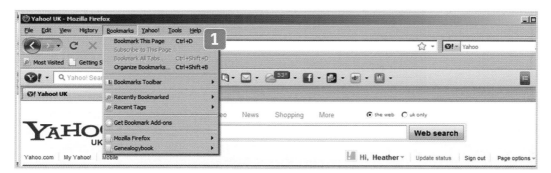

**2** Type the name of the site into the Page Bookmarked window that pops up.

**3** Click Done.

▶ **SEE ALSO:** The pages you bookmark will be available in your browser. Click Bookmark and scroll down to find your saved website.

🔥 **HOT TIP:** You can file your bookmarks in different folders when the Page Bookmarked window pops up. Choose a folder or create a folder with a name you will remember.

🔥 **HOT TIP:** You can label the website with words you are likely to remember when the Page Bookmarked window pops up: just type over the highlighted text.

# Use your browser's history

It is very common to either forget to bookmark a site or to navigate away from one and forget the exact name. Your browser will remember the sites that you have been on.

**1** Most browsers offer a History link. Click it.

**2** Select Show History (or Show All History depending on your browser).

**3** View the date you think you used the website you are looking for and click it (e.g. Yesterday, Last 7 days).

**4** Scroll through the links and double-click on the link you want.

**5** Scroll down the list of URLs to find the website you want.

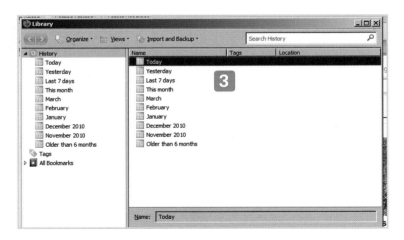

**HOT TIP:** You can click the Back arrow a few times to find websites you visited most recently.

**HOT TIP:** You can also put your cursor in the address bar and begin typing words you remember. Your browser will automatically provide you with a list of sites you have visited in the past.

# Stay safe on the internet

In the course of downloading files from the internet, you can inadvertently download a computer virus. Viruses can harm your computer or find personal information such as bank or credit details. Take the following precautions to keep your computer safe.

- Download AVG free. This is a type of free anti-virus software that you can save to your computer that will scan your computer regularly for malicious files.
- Don't open email from unknown senders.
- Don't download attachments from your email you weren't expecting (even if they are from a known sender).
- Keep your browser (Firefox, Internet Explorer, Google Chrome, Safari) up to date. These regular upgrades include improvements to keep you protected on the Internet.

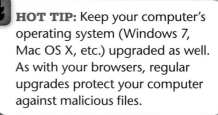

**HOT TIP:** You can set your computer to download updates to your browser automatically.

**HOT TIP:** Keep your computer's operating system (Windows 7, Mac OS X, etc.) upgraded as well. As with your browsers, regular upgrades protect your computer against malicious files.

# Create safe user names and passwords

As you begin to frequent the popular genealogy websites, you will be asked to create an account to use these sites. In order to create an account, you will need a user name and a password. A safe user name will consist of part of your name and some combination of numbers. Use the following tips to create a safe user name and password:

- Avoid using your full name to protect your identity. Instead, use part of your name or even an alias that will be easy for you to remember.
- Avoid using your birth date as part of the number combination.
- Don't use your email address as a user name.
- Don't use your email password as the password for your website account.
- Write down your password in a safe place away from your computer.
- Consider using a symbol in your password combination (i.e. Dav02*).

**Sign In**

User Name

Password

Sign In

Forgot your user name or password?

**? DID YOU KNOW?**
A locked padlock symbol on your web browser's address bar also shows you are on a secure site.

**! ALERT:** Make purchases online only when using a trusted website.

**WHAT DOES THIS MEAN?**
*S:* you will see an additional *s* in the URLs of some websites (https:). The *s* stands for secure and is there to show you are on a secure site.

# 3 Search census data

# Introduction

Census records for England, Wales and Scotland are widely available on the internet and contain a wealth of fascinating facts about your ancestors. The records for the Republic of Ireland and Northern Ireland are not as readily available, particularly prior to 1901. However, there is some information on the internet as well as a number of other ways you can find census information for relatives from these places.

# Understand census records

Census records are one of the most valuable sources of information for the family historian. Depending on the year, you find out where your relative was living, their occupation, and details about their children or others living in the household. With each census, new information was added to the form and the census became an even richer source of detail.

Some basic facts about the census:

- While census records began in 1801, the first census to record the names of every individual in the household was 1841.
- Many records from 1841 to 1911 are available online.
- After 1851, each individual's relationship to the head of the household is recorded.
- Most of the recently released census data from the 1911 census for England, Wales, the Channel Islands and the Isle of Man have been published online.

**? DID YOU KNOW?**
Certain information on the 1911 census is not due to be released until 2012. It includes information about a person's disability (see the Infirmity column).

**🔥 HOT TIP:** You can search census data for free on many websites but must pay for a scanned image of the record.

# Search the records at FreeCEN

This website is run entirely by volunteers with the goal of making genealogical data available to family researchers for free. They have transcribed many census records from 1841 to 1891. Some of these records have been fully transcribed and contain all of the information from the original census, including residence, occupation and details of household members.

**1** Go to www.freecen.org.uk.

**2** Click Search the database.

**3** Click the Year menu and select a census year to search.

**4** Enter the details for your relative, select a county or census place and click Find.

## UK Census Online

*"Bringing YOUR ancestors to YOU, free of charge!"*

Have YOU ever thought of the benefit of the U.K. Census data being centrally av

This project aims to provide a "free-to-view" online searchable database of the 19th century

**FreeCEN** is part of **FreeUKGEN**, an initiative aimed at helping make high quality primary (or search, information retrieval system.
Other projects associated with the FreeUKGEN initiative are **FreeBMD** and **FreeREG**.

**Volunteers**

Many volunteers world-wide are working on the transcription.

The number of volunteers has grown since its inception in 1999 to 125 in December 2000. It

We are constantly looking for new volunteers. We need help with Transcribing and Checkin volunteer to help with. To contact the Coordinator for a County that you are interested in he

As well as the 1891 Census we are also working on the 1841, 1851, 1861 and 1871 census. W page on http://www.freecen.org.uk/statistics.html

Please remember to keep coming back to check as we add more Census DATA.

**Search the Database**      **Information about Coverage**

Database last updated          **Database Coverage**
Friday, 18-Mar-2011 23:10:02 GMT   **Recent Additions**

On Mon 4 Apr 2011 FreeCEN users did
31,058 searches. (**Details**)

**2**

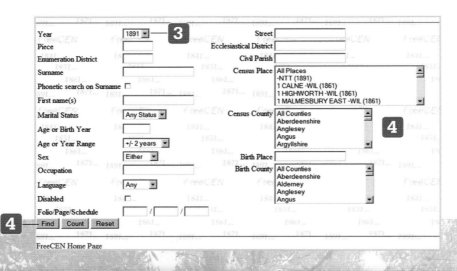

FreeCEN Home Page

---

**HOT TIP:** Save time by looking first at the statistics section of the website to see which censuses have been transcribed and added to the site.

**ALERT:** Keep this website bookmarked and check back often as they are constantly adding new census information to the site.

**5** Review the results for your family member and click Show Household to view the census information.

**6** Record the information into your family tree and make a note of the census record details.

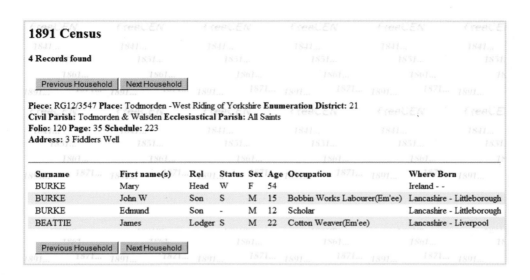

**1891 Census**

**4 Records found**

| Previous Household | Next Household |

**Piece:** RG12/3547 **Place:** Todmorden -West Riding of Yorkshire **Enumeration District:** 21
**Civil Parish:** Todmorden & Walsden **Ecclesiastical Parish:** All Saints
**Folio:** 120 **Page:** 35 **Schedule:** 223
**Address:** 3 Fiddlers Well

| Surname | First name(s) | Rel | Status | Sex | Age | Occupation | Where Born |
|---------|---------------|-----|--------|-----|-----|------------|------------|
| BURKE | Mary | Head | W | F | 54 | | Ireland - - |
| BURKE | John W | Son | S | M | 15 | Bobbin Works Labourer(Em'ee) | Lancashire - Littleborough |
| BURKE | Edmund | Son | - | M | 12 | Scholar | Lancashire - Littleborough |
| BEATTIE | James | Lodger | S | M | 22 | Cotton Weaver(Em'ee) | Lancashire - Liverpool |

| Previous Household | Next Household |

**SEE ALSO:** Don't be discouraged if you can't find your relatives on this index – there are many other sources of census data online.

**SEE ALSO:** www.scotlandspeople.gov.uk: this website contains more complete records of censuses from Scotland (for a fee).

# Search the census index on ancestry.co.uk

Ancestry.co.uk is a subscription website that contains a wealth of digitised, searchable historical records from government records, archives and other collections. In addition to scanning the original images into the database, all the material is indexed. You can search the indexes for free to see whether they contain any information about your relatives.

**1** Go to www.ancestry.co.uk.

**2** Click Search UK Census Records.

**3** Click Search now on the next screen.

> **⟨≣⟩ UK Census Records »**
>
> Explore the most comprehensive online collection of censuses from England, Wales and Scotland from 1841 - 1911. This archive is a great starting point for British family history:
>
> 1911 1901 1891 1881 1871 1861 1851 1841

**4** Enter the details for your relative in the fields and click Search.

**5** Scroll through the results to find your relative's record.

**6** Point your cursor over the green census index for a preview of the census record.

**HOT TIP:** *Do* on the original census records means *ditto*.

 **ALERT:** You will have to pay to view the full digital record.

▶ **SEE ALSO:** You can sign up for a pay as you go account if you want to view only a few images (about £7 for 12 images). See the next section for how to do this.

# Set up a pay-as-you-go account with ancestry.co.uk

While you are searching through the free indexes you may find you want to view one of the images. If you are not ready to set up an account or try the 14-day free trial, you can simply buy a set number of credits in order to view and print the records you want. This site makes it a little hard to use this option, so follow the steps below carefully. Setting up an account with Ancestry will be discussed in Chapter 6.

**1** Find a record you would like to view (from your previous searches).

**2** Click View Image.

**3** Click Pay As You Go.

**4** Select 12 record views for 14 days and click Continue.

**5** Enter your name and email address and click on terms and conditions (after reading them).

**6** Click Continue and you will be taken to a secure section of the site to buy your credits.

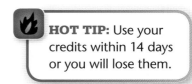

**HOT TIP:** Use your credits within 14 days or you will lose them.

**ALERT:** Tick or untick the boxes beneath your name after you have read the details. If they are all ticked, you may receive email solicitations you don't want.

**HOT TIP:** Devote one credit card to online purchases so you can easily monitor the charges you have accrued.

# Use advanced search options on ancestry.co.uk

Ancestry's database of census records contains so many records that you may find it difficult to locate your ancestor. You can refine your search if you are not getting the results you want or if you are getting too many results.

**1** Return to the free census section on ancestry.co.uk.

**2** Click Show Advanced.

**3** Enter your relative's approximate birth year.

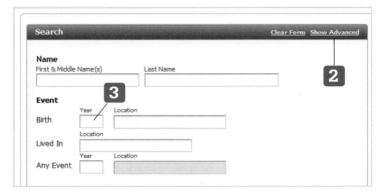

**4** Select a range (+/− 1, 2, 5 or 10 years).

**5** Click Search.

**6** If you still do not get the results you want:

- Change the variable (location, family member, etc.).
- Click Use default settings.
- Select the Restrict to option.
- Click Search.

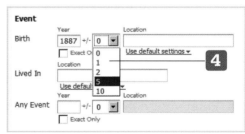

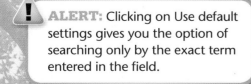

**ALERT:** Clicking on Use default settings gives you the option of searching only by the exact term entered in the field.

**HOT TIP:** Use a middle name or the initial of a middle name if you know it.

**HOT TIP:** Not all census sites have all the census data. Try more than one site if you are having trouble finding a record for your relative (see next section).

# Search 1911census.co.uk

FindMyPast was the first company to digitise and publish the 1911 census for England and Wales. It created this webpage to meet the needs of family historians who were keen to explore this most interesting of census records, released only in 2011.

1. Go to www.1911census.co.uk.

2. Enter your relative's details in the search form and click search.

3. Review the results to see if your relative is indexed on the site.

**Search the 1911 census**

* One of these fields must be used in every search.

| | |
|---|---|
| *First names | |
| *Last name | |
| Place of residence | |

See which areas are covered by the 1911 census. Register to get email updates.

Year of birth

Full person search
Search for a place — search — **2**

---

### 1911 census: person search results

3 results found. You searched for:

| First names | S |
|---|---|
| First names Algorithm | Exact |
| Last names | THOMPSON |
| Last names Algorithm | Exact |
| Residence | HACKNEY |

Is one of these the household you were searching for? You can now either view a transcript (new window) or an original household page (new window). To do this you will need to buy credits.

Search again

Transcripts are 10 credits and original pages are 30 credits. You will not be charged for transcripts or original pages that you have already purchased and are in your "my records".

| Schedule type | Last names | First names | Sex | Birth year | Age in 1911 | District / other | County / other | Transcript | Original page |
|---|---|---|---|---|---|---|---|---|---|
| HOUSEHOLD | THOMPSON | ALICE S | F | 1886 | 25 | Hackney | London | View Transcript (10 CREDITS) | View Original Page (30 CREDITS) |
| HOUSEHOLD | THOMPSON | H S | M | 1862 | 49 | Poplar | London | View Transcript (10 CREDITS) | View Original Page (30 CREDITS) |
| HOUSEHOLD | THOMPSON | REGINALD S | F | 1886 | 25 | Hackney | London | View Transcript (10 CREDITS) | View Original Page (30 CREDITS) |

Search again

about us   terms & conditions   privacy policy   copyright   accessibility   contact us   site map   search site   blog

---

▶ **SEE ALSO:** Click on View Original Page to purchase the image – see next section on how to do this.

**? DID YOU KNOW?**
This was the first census to contain details about a person's disability (see the Infirmity column). However, this data will not be released until 2012 or later.

**? DID YOU KNOW?**
The 1911 census was the first to include your relative's signature on the form.

# Buy credits on 1911census.co.uk

If you've found a record on the site that you want to view and save, you can sign into the website and purchase viewing credits. These credits can also be used on the sister site, FindMyPast.co.uk, which we will explore further in Chapter 4.

**1** Go to www.1911census.co.uk and click Buy credits.

**2** Enter your details in the fields and click Register.

**3** Click Skip to content, enter your relative's details and click Search.

**4** Click View Transcript for the record you want to view.

**5** Choose a payment option and click Continue.

## Choose a payment option

There are various payment packages for viewing the 1911 census. You can pay as you go on 1911census.co.uk, which could be a useful option if you are a beginner or if you just want to access a small number of records.

Transcripts cost 10 credits each and original pages cost 30 credits for the set of images.

○ **£6.95 - 60 credits** - £0.12 per credit expire 12 July 2011

○ **£24.95 - 280 credits** - £0.09 per credit expire 12 April 2012

**5**

payments powered by
RBS WorldPay

VISA    VISA    VISA    MasterCard    Maestro    ○    JCB

Continue

about us    terms & conditions    privacy policy    copyright    accessibility    contact us    site map    search site

**6** Once on the secure site, select the payment method.

**7** Enter your details in the fields and click Make Payment.

**ALERT:** Be aware that credits expire in 90 days. Buy only as many as you think you'll use to begin with.

**ALERT:** Viewing the original page provides you with an exact digital copy of the original record; the transcript is the basic information filled into the form (name, marital status, occupation) but costs less money.

**HOT TIP:** You can save your searched records on the site once you register.

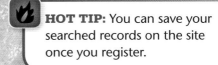

# Look for census data on FamilySearch

This site is part of the Church of Jesus Christ of Latter-Day Saints' (LDS) huge archive of genealogical information. LDS has one of the largest collections of genealogical data and has been slowly adding that information online. The website has a searchable database of the 1881 census for the UK. The major advantage of searching this site is that you get all the information contained on the 1881 census for free.

**1** Go to https://familysearch.org.

**2** Click on Europe.

**3** Scroll down to England and Wales Census, 1881 and click the link.

**4** Enter your relative's details and click Search.

**5** Click on the name to get a detailed record for your relative.

## England and Wales Census, 1881 for Charles Wiggett

« Back to search results

An image for this record may be available at: www.findmypast.co.uk Fees may apply.

- View image
- Search collection
- About this collection

name: Charles Wiggett
age: 16
gender: Male
birth year: 1865
birthplace: Bethnal Green, Middlesex, England
relationship to head of household: Son
marital condition: Single
profession/occupation: Box Maker
address: 38 Marian Square
census place: Bethnal Green, Middlesex, England
disability:
record type: Household
family history library film: 1341089
the national archives reference: RG11
piece/folio: 413 / 130
page number: 60

**5**

| Household | Gender | Age |
|---|---|---|
| parent George Wiggett | M | 43 |
| parent Sarah Wiggett | F | 37 |
| Elizabeth Wiggett | F | 18 |
| **Charles Wiggett** | M | 16 |
| Benjamin Wiggett | M | 13 |
| Emily Wiggett | F | 7 |
| Alice Wiggett | F | 4 |
| Anne Wiggett | F | 2 |
| Julia Stocker | F | 63 |
| Ada Stocker | F | 18 |
| Henry Hancock | M | 9 |

**! ALERT:** You will not get original record scans on this site but it does provide a detailed transcript of all the information contained on the 1881 census – for free.

**? DID YOU KNOW?** The only detailed records currently available on this site for the UK are for 1881. But you can still search the other censuses to see if your relative is there.

**! ALERT:** If you click on View original image it will take you to a fee-based partner website.

# Search the National Archives of Ireland

If you had ancestors from the Republic, you can search for free on the wonderful database created by the National Archives of Ireland. While many records prior to 1901 were destroyed, the site contains some of the most interesting census records on the web. The Irish census included more information about individuals than the English or Welsh ones, as well as information about the residents' dwellings and land.

**1** Go to www.census.nationalarchives.ie.

**2** Click Search the census records for Ireland 1901 and 1911.

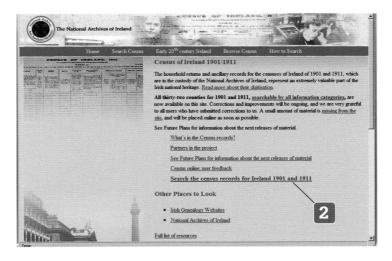

**3** Select a census year to search, enter your relative's details and click Search.

**4** Click on a record you want to view.

**5** Scroll down the page to View census images and click on the image link.

**6** Save the PDF file to your computer.

**? DID YOU KNOW?**
This site has a good collection of 1901 and 1911 census data for all 32 counties of Ireland.

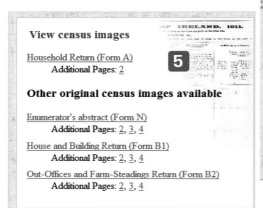

**! ALERT:** Click the links to Forms B1 and B2 beneath the census link. They contain interesting additional information about the dwelling and other structures found on farms.

**? DID YOU KNOW?**
The Irish census has a section that contains information about the individual's ability to read and write as well as a section about their ability to speak Irish, English, or both.

**! ALERT:** Remember to vary the spelling of your search if you don't get the results you are looking for (O'Leary, Leary, Lery, etc.).

# Save your ancestors' census records

Many of the sites included in this chapter do not offer documents in PDF format. You will have the option of printing them from the sites but you probably want to save the image for your records, especially if it is very detailed. If the site does not offer you a way to save your file, do the following to save it to your computer.

**1** Right-click on the image you want to save.

**2** Select Save Page As.

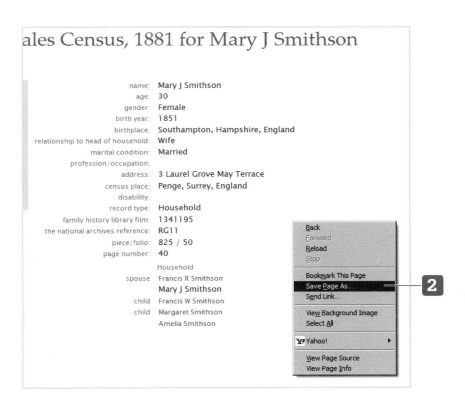

### ales Census, 1881 for Mary J Smithson

| | |
|---|---|
| name: | Mary J Smithson |
| age: | 30 |
| gender: | Female |
| birth year: | 1851 |
| birthplace: | Southampton, Hampshire, England |
| relationship to head of household: | Wife |
| marital condition: | Married |
| profession/occupation: | |
| address: | 3 Laurel Grove May Terrace |
| census place: | Penge, Surrey, England |
| disability: | |
| record type: | Household |
| family history library film: | 1341195 |
| the national archives reference: | RG11 |
| piece/folio: | 825 / 50 |
| page number: | 40 |
| | Household |
| spouse | Francis R Smithson |
| | Mary J Smithson |
| child | Francis W Smithson |
| child | Margaret Smithson |
| | Amelia Smithson |

Back
Forward
Reload
Stop

Bookmark This Page
Save Page As...
Send Link...

View Background Image
Select All

Yahoo!

View Page Source
View Page Info

**2**

 **ALERT:** The file will be saved as a webpage. When you open it from your computer it will come up as a webpage but one that you can view offline.

 **HOT TIP:** Click on the when you see it on a site to save the file.

**3** Name the file.

**4** Select a folder on your computer where you want to keep the file.

**5** Click Save.

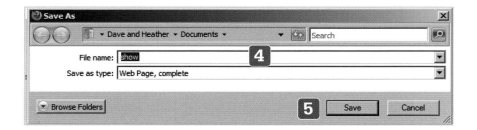

**ALERT:** Some webpages will charge for saving their records.

# 4 Find birth, marriage and death information

# Introduction

In the last chapter, you were able to locate family information in the cenus data. In this chapter, you can find out specific details of individuals within the family. Birth, marriage and death registries are records kept by the General Register Office of England and Wales. With the details you will find in the registers, you can pinpoint a person in a time and place, and gather the details needed to order copies of their original birth, marriage or death certificates. Also explored in the chapter are the parish records available online for baptisms, marriages and burials – mostly prior to 1837.

# Search for records on FreeBMD

This website is run by the same volunteers who run the FreeCEN site mentioned in the last chapter. It has more than 200 million records transcribed and linked to the site, with an excellent number of records for the years 1837–1929. This should be your first stop when looking for free BMD information on the web. The database is updated every month.

**1** Go to www.freebmd.org.uk and click Search.

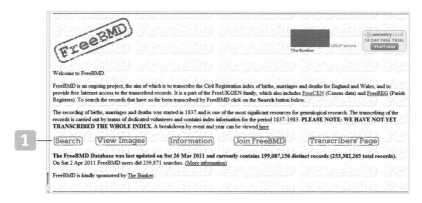

**2** Select the type of records you are looking for (i.e. all births, marriages, deaths).

**3** Enter the details for your relative and select district if you know it.

**4** Select a county to search.

**5** Choose a date range that covers at least two years.

**6** Click Find.

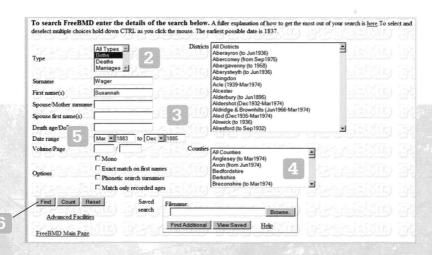

**7** Click Revise Query if you don't find a record you were looking for.

 **ALERT:** You must select a county or the search will not function.

**ALERT:** Write down the full citation, including district, volume and page.

**HOT TIP:** Some records have an image of the original record linked to them. Click the glasses icon  where you see it to view.

**SEE ALSO:** A more complete set of BMD records and parish data for Scotland is available at www.scotlandspeople.gov.uk. The site charges a fee to view records but it is an excellent source of family history data for anyone with roots in Scotland.

# Look for BMD records on familysearch.org

There are a number of BMD records on the FamilySearch site, with more being added frequently. The index spans from the 1700s to the mid-1900s, though some counties are better represented than others, and it is not yet a comprehensive set of records. But it is worth looking here before searching other databases as you can search and view the information for free.

**1** Go to https://familysearch.org, scroll down the page and click Europe.

**2** Scroll down to the links for BMD records for England and select a link.

**3** Enter the details for your relative and click Search.

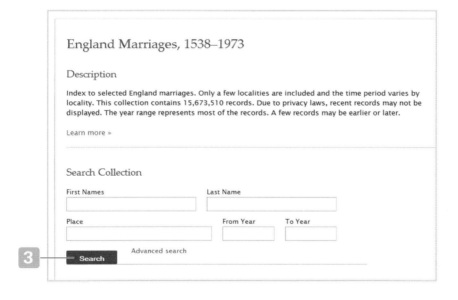

England Marriages, 1538–1973

Description

Index to selected England marriages. Only a few localities are included and the time period varies by locality. This collection contains 15,673,510 records. Due to privacy laws, recent records may not be displayed. The year range represents most of the records. A few records may be earlier or later.

Learn more »

Search Collection

First Names

Last Name

Place

From Year

To Year

**3** — Search       Advanced search

**ALERT:** The FamilySearch site contains parish information as well as the information from the GRO.

**HOT TIP:** If too many search results are returned, tick the Match all exactly box and re-enter details for your relative to run the search again.

**4** Scroll through the results and click a name to view.

| | |
|---|---|
| groom's name: | **George Walker** |
| groom's birth date: | 1849 |
| groom's birthplace: | |
| groom's age: | 22 |
| bride's name: | Sarah Jane Hopkins |
| bride's birth date: | 1847 |
| bride's birthplace: | |
| bride's age: | 24 |
| marriage date: | 07 May 1871 |
| marriage place: | Kidderminster, Worcester, England |
| groom's father's name: | John Walker |
| groom's mother's name: | |
| bride's father's name: | |
| bride's mother's name: | |
| groom's race: | |
| groom's marital status: | |
| groom's previous wife's name: | |
| bride's race: | |
| bride's marital status: | |
| bride's previous husband's name: | |
| indexing project (batch) number: | I02913-9 |
| system origin: | England-EASy |
| source film number: | 1040277 |
| reference number: | v 13 p 92 |

**5** Write down the details if you think the record matches your relative.

**HOT TIP:** Record the sites you have visited and the information you have found on each site.

# Search for parish records on FreeREG

This is another great site by the UKGen team that contains a searchable database of baptism, marriage and burial information from a range of parishes in the UK.

**1** Go to www.freereg.org.uk.

**2** Click Search Parish Registers, then click search now.

> **!** **ALERT:** You can select All for the place but you must select a county for the Search to function.

FreeREG stands for Free REGisters.

Our objective is to provide free Internet searches of baptism, marriage, and burial records, that have been transcribed from parish and non-conformist re to **FreeBMD** (a database of the GRO birth, marriage and death indexes from 1837) and **FreeCEN** (a database of census information).

We are in need of volunteers willing to transcribe registers, to make their existing transcriptions available on FreeREG or undertake one of the many su information on how to participate.)

The FreeREG database contains 2,747,887 Marriages, 7,680,421 Baptisms and 4,750,293 Burials. The last update started on Fri 11 Mar 2011 and was completed on

On Sun 3 Apr 2011 FreeREG users did 24,816 searches. (Details)

**2** — Search Parish Registers   What is FreeREG?   How to Volunteer   Information for Transcribers   Counties and Parishes

**3** Select a record type (baptism, marriage, burial).

**4** Enter your relative's details (choose a county or place) and click search.

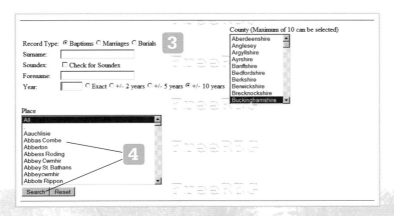

> **?** **DID YOU KNOW?**
> Birth registers did not contain the mother's maiden name until after 1911.

> **▶** **SEE ALSO:** There are a number of websites explored in this chapter because no one website seems to contain all of the BMD information, so it is worth looking at more than one.

# Register and buy credits with BMDIndex.co.uk

This site is run by TheGenealogist.co.uk, a subscription-based family research site. It offers a very reasonably priced option for searching through a number of BMDs from 1837–2005. It also claims a large number of non-parochial records.

Do the following to buy credits to view the records.

**1** Go to www.bmdindex.co.uk.

**2** Click the Credit-based access to BMD Index 1837–2005 link.

**3** Choose a subscription type and click Add to Basket.

**4** Tick I have read the terms and conditions link (after doing so).

**5** Click Checkout.

**6** Enter your details in the fields and click Submit.

**7** Enter your payment details and click Submit payment.

**8** Click Complete payment.

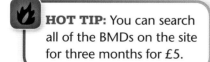

**HOT TIP:** You can search all of the BMDs on the site for three months for £5.

**DID YOU KNOW?** BMD data are also referred to as vital records.

**ALERT:** Don't click on the Submit payment button more than once – doing so could alter or cancel your transaction.

**SEE ALSO:** No one site has comprehensive information for non-conformist relatives. With a Gold or Diamond Premium subscription to The Genealogist or with the purchase of credits at BMDRegisters.co.uk, you can search for your non-conformist relatives on each of these sites.

# Look for records on BMDIndex.co.uk

Now that you have credits to view records on the site, write down the names and approximate dates for the people you are interested in researching.

**1** Check you are on the *Research View* section of the website.

**2** Click the Click to SEARCH link and select a search option on the next page.

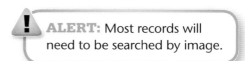 **ALERT:** Most records will need to be searched by image.

TheGenealogist.co.uk homepage. www.TheGenealogist.co.uk

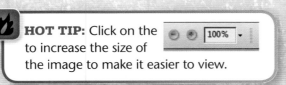 **HOT TIP:** Click on the to increase the size of the image to make it easier to view.

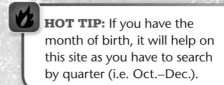 **HOT TIP:** If you have the month of birth, it will help on this site as you have to search by quarter (i.e. Oct.–Dec.).

3 Select the records to search and enter your relative's details.

4 Click a link to a year and quarter that may contain your relative.

5 Scan the document to find your relative's details and write them down.

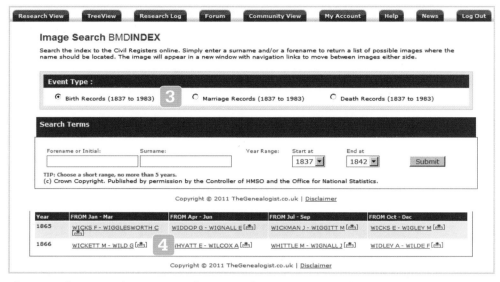

The Genealogist.co.uk image search BMD index screen, www.TheGenealogist.co.uk

**DID YOU KNOW?**
The images on this site are kept as PDF files and are easy to download, save and open on your computer.

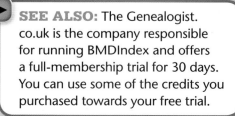

**SEE ALSO:** The Genealogist.co.uk is the company responsible for running BMDIndex and offers a full-membership trial for 30 days. You can use some of the credits you purchased towards your free trial.

# Look for BMDs on ancestry.co.uk

If you have credit from a pay-as-you-go account on this site, you can search any of its records, including BMD registers and parish information. If you haven't set up this type of account, see Chapter 3 for information on how to do this. The advantage of this site is that it has complete records for the period 1916–2005, so you will be able to find information for your most recent relatives.

> **ALERT:** You may be required to register as a free user. All you will need to do is provide your name (can be an alias) and your email address.

1. Go to www.ancestry.co.uk and click on Birth, Marriage and Death Indexes.

2. Choose a collection and year to search through.

3. Enter your relative's details, choose a date range and include any other information you know.

4. Click Search.

5. Click on View Record for details of the register you searched for.

6. Write down the registration details (quarter, volume, page) for your records.

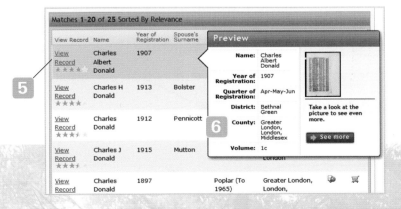

> **ALERT:** You will be charged a fee for the records from 1916–2005.

> **HOT TIP:** You can also preview the record by holding your cursor over the View Record link.

# Search for BMDs on findmypast.co.uk

If you didn't purchase credits to view census records at www.1911census.co.uk in the last chapter, consider doing so now to view BMD data. The two sites are run by the same company and you can use the account information (name and password) you used on the census site. As with their census site, you can search for free but need to pay to view the original record image.

**1** Go to www.findmypast.co.uk/BirthsMarriagesDeaths.jsp.

**2** Click Search on a set of records you want to explore.

| Deaths & Burials | Search | PayAsYouGo Credits | Subscriptions |
|---|---|---|---|
| England and Wales 1837-1983 | Search ▶ | 1 | Foundation & Full |
| England and Wales 1984-2006 | **2** Search ▶ | 5 | Foundation & Full |
| British overseas 1761-1994 | Search ▶ | 1 | Foundation & Full |
| British overseas 1995-2005 | Search ▶ | 5 | Foundation & Full |
| Deaths at sea 1854-1890 | Search ▶ | 3 | Foundation & Full |
| Parish burials 1538-2005 | Search ▶ | 5 - 10 | Full |
| Probate & Wills 1462-1858 | Search ▶ | 5 - 10 | Full |

**3** Enter the details for your relative and click Search.

**4** Scan the results for your relative if you have more than one result.

**5** Click View on the image you want to view.

**HOT TIP:** Click Sign in if you have created an account already with www.1911census.co.uk.

**ALERT:** Most views of BMD records will cost you between one and ten credits, depending on the record.

**6** Click print page or write down the information for your records.

**DID YOU KNOW?**
This site allows you to search for both spouses on a marriage certificate at the same time.

**SEE ALSO:** This site has a good collection of searchable parish information (baptisms, marriages and burials) in addition to the BMD registers.

# Buy certificates on the GRO website

With the details you found on the BMD sites, you can now buy a copy of an original birth, marriage or death certificate. Having copies of these documents can help move your research forward and add to your growing documentation of your family's lives. You will need all the information included on the BMD registry records (name, surname, district, volume and page number).

**1** Go to www.gro.gov.uk/gro/content/certificates and click Order a certificate online now.

**2** Click the Registration link.

**3** Enter your details and click Submit.

> ⚠ **ALERT:** You have to register first to place an order on the site.

**4** Select a certificate type.

**5** Select Yes next to Is the GRO Index Reference Number known?

**6** Enter the year of the event in the box and click Submit.

Certificate Types **4**

For events registered in England and Wales

1. Birth Certificate (England & Wales) ○
2. Marriage Certificate (England & Wales) ○
3. Civil Partnership Certificate (England & Wales) ○
4. Death Certificate (England & Wales) ○ Age at death in years [     ]
5. Adoption Certificate (England & Wales) ○ Current age of adoptee [     ]
6. Commemorative Marriage Certificate (England & Wales) ○

For overseas events which were registered with the British authorities

7. Birth Certificate (Overseas events) ○
8. Marriage Certificate (Overseas events) ○
9. Civil Partnership Certificate (Overseas events) ○
10. Death Certificate (Overseas events) ○ Age at death in years [     ]

For Death Applications

Age at death must be given for applications where event was registered in the last 50 years.

For all events

Is the GRO Index Reference Number known? (Explanation)  Yes ⦿  No ○ **5**

Year in which the event was registered
(If you aren't supplying a GRO Reference and don't know
the exact date of event you can enter a year to be searched
- we will search the specified year and one either side) [     ] **6**

**7** Confirm your information and click Submit.

**8** Enter your relative's details, choose a delivery option and click Submit.

**9** Click Checkout to pay or Add to order to add another record.

**! ALERT:** You can enter information for only one certificate at a time in the online form.

**? DID YOU KNOW?** You can opt for priority service for a fee and have the document mailed the next day.

# Buy certificates for the Republic of Ireland and Northern Ireland

There are no records of births, deaths and marriages currently available online for the Republic of Ireland or Northern Ireland. However, there are a number of things you can do to trace your ancestors from these areas, including purchasing copies of their vital records at a registry office.

- For the Republic of Ireland you will need the family name, approximate date of birth, marriage or death, and the parish or townland they lived in.
- For Northern Ireland you need the family name, approximate dates and the district information or the full address.
- Roman Catholic records are available through the GRO of Ireland from 1864 onwards – www.groireland.ie.
- The Office of the Registrar General has marriage records from 1845–1864 and all non-Catholic registerable marriages thereafter.

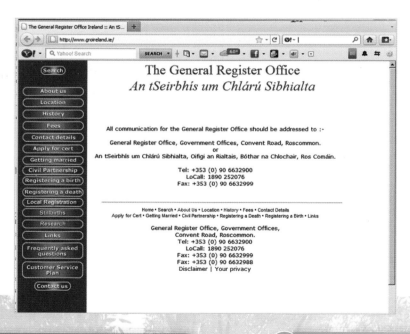

**SEE ALSO:** Make sure that you have looked at the National Archives of Ireland website for the 1901 and 1911 census information for your family (see Chapter 3 for information on how to do this).

**? DID YOU KNOW?** A townland, also called a bally, is a small division of land in Ireland.

- Parish records prior to 1864 are held in most local parishes and include baptism, marriage and burial information.
- Non-Catholic records are available in both the GRO of Ireland (until 1922) and the GRO of Northern Ireland from 1845 to the present – see www.nidirect.gov.uk/gro.

# 5 Explore the National Archives

# Introduction

The National Archives is a wonderful repository of original documents from more than 1,000 years of UK history. Over the last several years, millions of original government records have been scanned and digitised, and made available to the public online. There are searchable databases and indexes of the documents, many of significant interest to genealogists. The tasks in this chapter should enable you to negotiate your way around the website and find valuable information about your relatives.

# Learn what the Archives have to offer

The Archives has a large documents online section of interest to the family historian, including an index of wills, government papers and military records. By far the greatest resource on the site is the wealth of military records available to download. If you had ancestors in a branch of the military, particularly the navy, this site will be of great interest to you.

Some of the records you will find include the following:

- Wills before 1858, mostly related to residents in southern England.
- Death duty registers for England and Wales from 1796 to 1903.
- Royal Air Force records including officers' service records and Campaign Medal Index cards.
- Royal Marine records, including service records from 1842 to 1936 and Royal Naval Officers' service records.
- Army records, including Medal cards for the First World War and Victoria Cross registers.

**ALERT:** You will be charged a fee of £2–4 for downloading many of the documents, but you can search them for free.

 **HOT TIP:** The National Archives regularly puts new records on the site. Check back often to see what has been added.

 **SEE ALSO:** If you did not have military ancestors, search through the Looking for a Person? section of the website for valuable links and information of interest to the genealogist: www.nationalarchives.gov.uk/records/looking-for-person/default.htm

# Create a MyPage account

A MyPage account is a personal page on the site where you can save information. You can save searches you've done by creating bookmarks to your MyPage account. You can save up to 30 searches this way which can be accessed each time you log into your MyPage account.

1. Go to: www.nationalarchives.gov.uk.

2. Click on the MyPage link in the upper right corner of the site.

3. Click on Create a MyPage Account.

**HOT TIP:** There is a staggering amount of historical information in the National Archives site – not all of it relevant to the family historian. Use your MyPage account to save the searches you want to remember.

**ALERT:** You must be logged into your MyPage account to have access to saved bookmarks.

**4** Enter your details in the three steps (pages). Click Next step after completing each page.

**5** Click on I have read and agree to the terms of use and privacy statement (after doing so).

**6** Type in the security code.

**7** Click Register now.

**? DID YOU KNOW?**

Once you sign up for a MyPage account, the site will suggest useful links for you based on your searches.

# Identify your family member's service details

Many of the service records in the Archives are not indexed by the individual's birth date. Try to find as many details about their service as possible to aid your search.

- Name – search by last name and first initial.
- Service dates – search the dates of service, date of discharge or date of death.
- Army – identify the corps or regiment.
- Rank – uncover the rank: include private, sergeant, corporal, driver, gunner, major, etc.
- Air Force – look for squadron or division information.
- Navy – find the name of the ship served on or the company number to help find division information.

**ALERT:** Before 1873, many of the soldiers' records are arranged by Regiment.

**? DID YOU KNOW?**
Sergeant was spelled serjeant in many Archive documents from the First and Second World Wars.

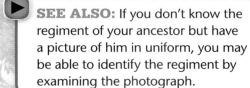

**SEE ALSO:** If you don't know the regiment of your ancestor but have a picture of him in uniform, you may be able to identify the regiment by examining the photograph.

# Search the army records

The site has many army records of interest to the family historian, including the Campaign Medal Index cards, Victoria Cross registers and Recommendations for Honours and Awards. Campaign medals were awarded to almost all who saw active service overseas. The Archives have copies of the Index cards with the basic information about the individual and the type of honour awarded.

**1** Go to www.nationalarchives.gov.uk/documentsonline/army.asp.

**2** Click on the Search link under the heading for Campaign Medal Index Cards, First World War.

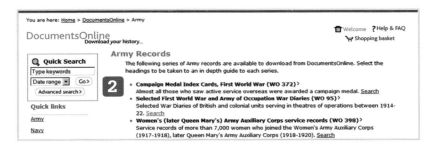

**3** Enter your relative's information in the First Name and Last Name fields.

**4** Enter any other information you have gathered and click Search.

**5** Scroll through the document results for your relative.

**6** Click Refine Search if you don't get the information you were looking for.

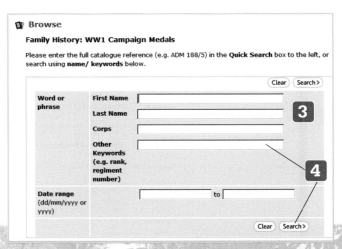

▶ **SEE ALSO:** See the 'Order a document online' section of this chapter for information on how to purchase and download documents from the National Archives website.

**! ALERT:** Many of the army service records were destroyed during a bombing raid in 1940.

# Search the navy records

The naval records are some of the most comprehensive on the site. There are service records for a vast array of naval divisions, including the Royal Marines, Royal Naval Seamen, Royal Naval Officers, Royal Naval Reserve and the Women's Royal Naval Service during the First World War. Of particular interest on these forms is the amount of personal detail recorded. Many note a person's physical description, birth place, occupation prior to service and religion, in addition to details of their service.

1 Go to www.nationalarchives.gov.uk/ documentsonline/navy.asp.

2 Click the search link beneath the Royal Marines Service Records or click another set of records that interests you.

3 Enter as much information as you know about your relative in the fields provided.

4 Click Search.

5 Scroll through the document results for your relative.

---

**Family History: Royal Marines Register of Service**

52 documents found

Displaying documents: 1 to 10

Refine search >

page 1 2 3 4 5 6 ⊙

| Description ⌄ | | Date ⌄ | Catalogue ref | Details |
|---|---|---|---|---|
| Name | Williams, Thomas Edwin | 08 August 1907 | ADM 159/173 | See details > |
| Register Number: | 22426 | | | |
| Division: | Royal Marine Light Infantry: Plymouth Division | | | |
| When Enlisted/Date of Enlistment: | 18 September 1924 | | | |
| Name | Williams, Thomas Edwin | 08 August 1907 | ADM 159/142 | See details > |
| Register Number: | 24845 | | | |
| Division: | Royal Marine Light Infantry: Chatham Division | | | |
| When Enlisted/Date of Enlistment: | 18 September 1924 | | | |
| Name | Williams, George Thomas | 06 February 1904 | ADM 159/91 | See details > |
| Register Number: | 15593 | | | |

---

**Image details**

+ Add to shopping

| Description | Name | Williams, Thomas Edwin |
|---|---|---|
| | Register Number: | 22426 |
| | Division: | Royal Marine Light Infantry: Plymouth Division |
| | When Enlisted/Date of Enlistment: | 18 September 1924 |

**Date** 08 August 1907

**Catalogue reference** ADM 159/173

**Dept** Records of the Admiralty, Naval Forces, Royal Marines, Coastguard, and related bodies

**Series** Admiralty: Royal Marines: Registers of Service

**Piece** 22367 - 22603

**Image contains** 1 document of many for this catalogue reference.

Number of image files: 1

| Image Reference | Format and Version | Part Number | Size (KB) | Number of Pages | Price (£) |
|---|---|---|---|---|---|
| 60 / 60 | PDF 1.2 | 1 | 191 | 1 | 3.50 |

| Total Price (£) | | | | | 3.50 |

< Return to search results            + Add to shopping

---

**? DID YOU KNOW?**

You can search and download the service registers of about 110,000 individuals who joined the Royal Marines between 1842 and 1925.

**🔥 HOT TIP:** There are thousands of records for women who served with the Women's Royal Naval Service from 1917–1919.

# Search the air force records

The Archives hold the service details for approximately 27,000 officers who served in the First World War. Information on the records includes the officer's full name, date and place of birth as well as next of kin. If one of your family members served as an officer in the RAF during the First World War, you can download a truly useful piece of family history.

**1** Go to www.nationalarchives.gov.uk/documentsonline/airforce.asp.

**2** Click on the Search link beneath the Royal Air Force officers' service records.

**3** Enter the details of your relative's name and service dates and click Search.

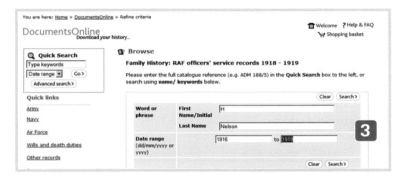

**4** Click See details to browse the record you are interested in.

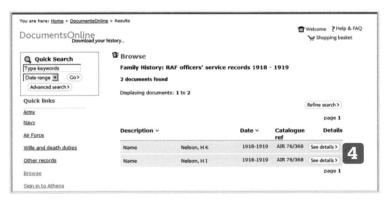

**ALERT:** Some records have only the initials of the officer's first name. Try limiting your search in the name field to the first letter of the individual's first name.

**SEE ALSO:** Take a look at the Women's Royal Air Force (WRAF) records. There are searchable service records for around 30,000 women who served during the First World War.

# Order a document online (Medal card)

Some of the most popular and interesting documents for download on the site are the Medal Index cards for the First World War. There are more than 5 million of them on the site. The cards contain information about the individual's medal entitlement, rank, unit and sometimes the first theatre of war in which they served.

**1** Go to the DocumentsOnline section of the website and click Medal Cards.

**2** Click Search under the heading for What is the Medal Rolls Index?

**3** Locate a Medal card you want to download.

**4** Click Add to shopping, then click Checkout.

**HOT TIP:** You can order and download any of the documents online (for wills, naval, army and Air Force records) using the same steps above.

**5** Enter your information and credit card details.

**6** Click Download my documents now either on the page or through your email.

**7** Save your documents to your computer.

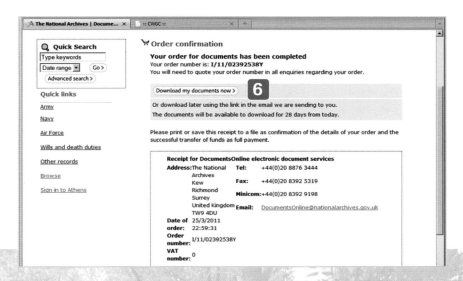

**! ALERT:** The document you order will be available for download for only 28 days after you place your order.

**! ALERT:** You will be sent a receipt in your email with the details of your order. Save this email for future reference if you don't download the document immediately.

# Search the Commonwealth War Graves Commission database

While not part of the National Archives itself, the Commonwealth War Graves Commission (CWGC) database is an excellent source of information about your relative who fought and died in the First or Second World War. The Debt of Honour Register contains a searchable index of 1.7 million men who died while serving in the two wars. Information in the database includes name, regiment, rank, age at death as well as additional information about their residence and next of kin.

**1** Go to www.cwgc.org.

**2** Click Search our Records.

**3** Enter the details for your relative and click Submit.

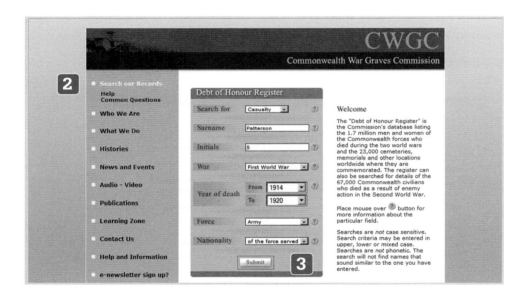

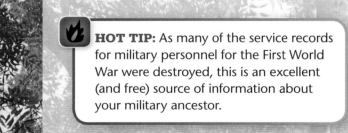

**HOT TIP:** As many of the service records for military personnel for the First World War were destroyed, this is an excellent (and free) source of information about your military ancestor.

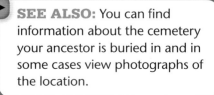

**SEE ALSO:** You can find information about the cemetery your ancestor is buried in and in some cases view photographs of the location.

4  If you see an index of names, search for your relative's name and click on it.

5  Note the details in your records or for further research.

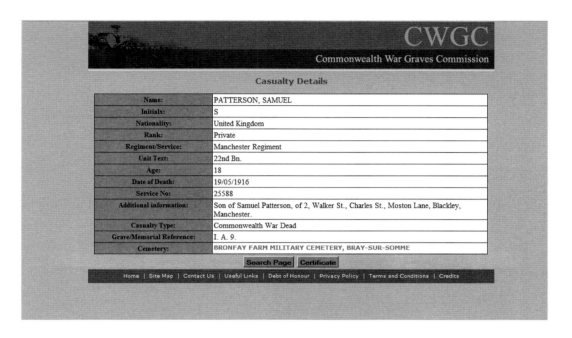

| | |
|---|---|
| **Name:** | PATTERSON, SAMUEL |
| **Initials:** | S |
| **Nationality:** | United Kingdom |
| **Rank:** | Private |
| **Regiment/Service:** | Manchester Regiment |
| **Unit Text:** | 22nd Bn. |
| **Age:** | 18 |
| **Date of Death:** | 19/05/1916 |
| **Service No:** | 25588 |
| **Additional information:** | Son of Samuel Patterson, of 2, Walker St., Charles St., Moston Lane, Blackley, Manchester. |
| **Casualty Type:** | Commonwealth War Dead |
| **Grave/Memorial Reference:** | I. A. 9. |
| **Cemetery:** | BRONFAY FARM MILITARY CEMETERY, BRAY-SUR-SOMME |

CWGC
Commonwealth War Graves Commission

Casualty Details

Search Page   Certificate

Home | Site Map | Contact Us | Useful Links | Debt of Honour | Privacy Policy | Terms and Conditions | Credits

# Search the wills

The records available for download consist of wills of mostly wealthy individuals from the south of England and Wales (1384–1858) from the Prerogative Court of Canterbury (PCC). The PCC was the most senior church court. Until 1858, wills had to be approved and recognised through the PCC. The Archives also contains a collection of wills from 35,000 Royal Naval seamen from 1786–1882.

**1** Go to www.nationalarchives.gov.uk/documentsonline/seamenswills.asp (Royal Naval Seamen) or to www.nationalarchives.gov.uk/documentsonline/wills.asp (wills proved at the PCC).

**2** Click Search under the heading.

**3** Enter your family member's details and click Search.

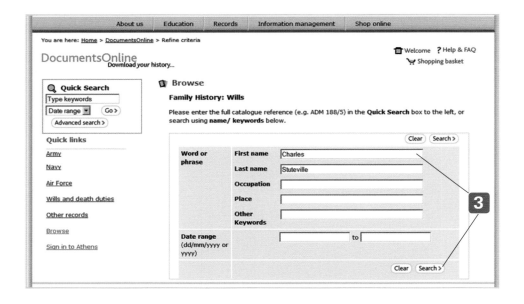

**HOT TIP:** Wills can help you to uncover not only details of a person's property but a description of the person, the names of family members and how the estate was divided.

**SEE ALSO:** There are many other subscription websites that contain searchable databases of later wills and wills for other areas of England and Wales, which we will explore later in the book.

**4** Select the abstract that matches the details for your relative and click See details.

**5** Click Add to shopping if you want to buy and download the document (see directions above).

**6** Click Save As, name the file and save the file to your computer.

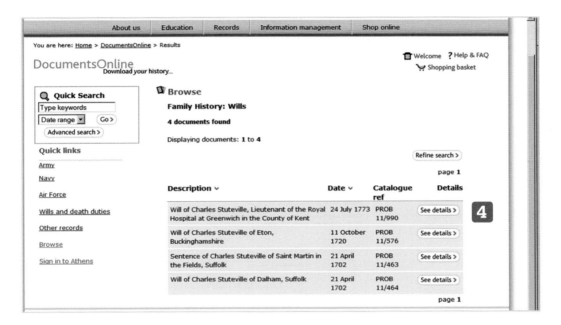

**? DID YOU KNOW?**

The National Archives has an online tutorial to help you decipher old handwriting in wills and other documents – see www.nationalarchives.gov.uk/palaeography.

# Explore death duty registers

Death duties were taxes charged to an estate worth a certain amount of money. The registers at the National Archives contain records for the dates 1796–1903. Similar to wills, the records can help you discover the name, location and occupation of your relative, what their estate may have been worth, the names of family members as well as the amount of tax paid. Significantly, the registers hold the details of individuals from a more diverse socioeconomic background, including tradesmen and other skilled workers.

**1** Go to www.nationalarchives.gov.uk/documentsonline/death-duty.asp.

**2** Click Search and enter the names and dates of your relative.

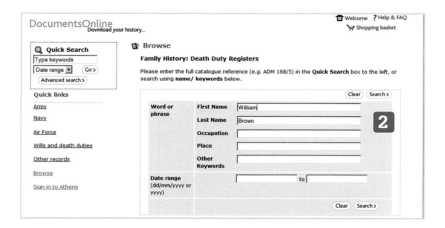

**3** Select the abstract that matches the details for your relative and click See details.

**4** Click Add to shopping if you want to buy and download the document (see directions above).

**5** Click Save As, name the file and save the file to your computer.

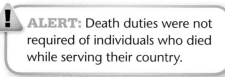

**ALERT:** Death duties were not required of individuals who died while serving their country.

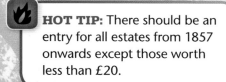

**HOT TIP:** There should be an entry for all estates from 1857 onwards except those worth less than £20.

**DID YOU KNOW?**

The death duty registers could be annotated for years after their creation and can contain information about the death of a spouse, death or marriage of beneficiaries and reference to law suits against the estate.

# Search the Trafalgar Ancestors database

This online exhibition contains a database with biographical information about the 18,000 individuals who fought with the Royal Navy in the Battle of Trafalgar. It draws on several sources, including the National Archives Admiralty records, the ships' musters, service registers and Greenwich Hospital records, among others.

**1** Go to www.nationalarchives.gov.uk/nelson.

**2** Click Find your Trafalgar ancestor, enter a last name and click Search.

**3** Browse the records to find your relative and click More.

**4** Write down the details and note the reference information.

**? DID YOU KNOW?**

If your relative served in the Royal Navy in 1805, there is a chance that they served during the Battle of Trafalgar.

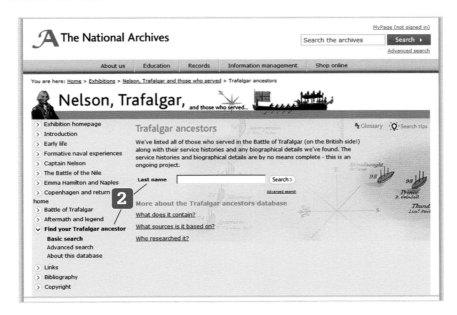

**🔥 HOT TIP:** You can narrow your search by clicking on Advanced search and search by your relative's approximate age, birth place, ship's name or rank.

**? DID YOU KNOW?**

The individuals who fought with Nelson came from remarkably diverse backgrounds – some were born in Africa, America, the West Indies and India. There is even good evidence of one woman who served during the battle.

# 6 Trace family migrants

# Introduction

The UK has a long history of migration; both individuals who came from another country to settle in the UK and those who left to start anew in a different country. Tracing these ancestors can be a challenge as at this time there is no one website that contains comprehensive records for the United Kingdom. You will have to do a bit of digging around to find information and other clues about your relative's travels, particularly if they travelled to and from non Commonwealth countries or countries outside of Europe.

The first half of the chapter will focus on how to find information for your immigrant ancestors while the second half will focus on those relatives who left the UK for other locations.

# Learn about immigration sources

Immigrants have travelled to the UK throughout its history, but immigration increased dramatically in the 19th century. Many of the best records are for that period and come in the form of passenger lists. Below are some sources of information about immigration to the UK.

- Incoming passenger lists. The Board of Trade kept separate records for British passengers and alien passengers.
- Certificates of alien arrivals and returns. These documents contain information about non-British citizens arriving in England during the 19th century.
- Alien registration cards. After 1914, aliens were required to register with the police.
- Aliens' entry books. A collection of correspondence and other documents from the Home Office and the Aliens Office.

**ALERT:** Try to locate the following information before searching passenger lists and arrival records: country of origin, how they travelled, place (city/port) of arrival and date of arrival.

 **SEE ALSO:** At this time alien registration cards for London can be searched only on the National Archives website. No other registration cards are available online.

# Find immigration information on ancestry.co.uk

Ancestry.co.uk has the Incoming Passengers lists from 1878–1960, as well as passenger lists for other ports outside the UK. You can use your pay-as-you-go credits to search the immigration records if you already have them or buy more credits (to use within 14 days). See Chapter 3 for information on how to buy credits.

**1** Go to www.ancestry.co.uk.

**2** Click the Immigration link.

**3** Enter your relative's details and click Search.

**4** Click on the document type to see a summary.

**5** Click View Image to see the scan of the original image.

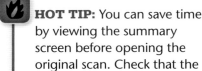

**HOT TIP:** You can save time by viewing the summary screen before opening the original scan. Check that the information matches that for your relative, i.e. approximate age and port of departure.

**6** Click Print to print a copy for your files.

**ALERT:** Much of the data for the passenger arrivals collection is from countries in Europe.

**SEE ALSO:** Chapter 7 has information on how to choose a subscription to join Ancestry.co.uk.

# Explore movinghere.org.uk

This site documents and examines the experiences of immigrants coming to the UK over the last 200 years. It offers practical advice on how to research your relatives from the Caribbean, Ireland, Southern Asia as well as those of Jewish descent. There are also links to sources of original records to help with your search.

1. Go to www.movinghere.org.uk.

2. Click Tracing Your Roots.

3. Click a community to research.

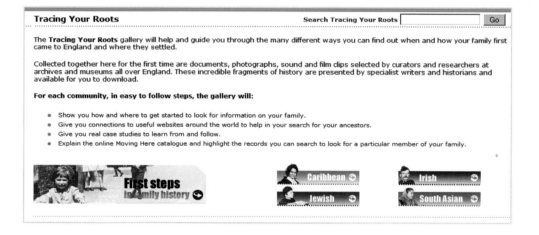

**Tracing Your Roots**      Search Tracing Your Roots [      ] [ Go ]

The **Tracing Your Roots** gallery will help and guide you through the many different ways you can find out when and how your family first came to England and where they settled.

Collected together here for the first time are documents, photographs, sound and film clips selected by curators and researchers at archives and museums all over England. These incredible fragments of history are presented by specialist writers and historians and available for you to download.

**For each community, in easy to follow steps, the gallery will:**

- Show you how and where to get started to look for information on your family.
- Give you connections to useful websites around the world to help in your search for your ancestors.
- Give you real case studies to learn from and follow.
- Explain the online Moving Here catalogue and highlight the records you can search to look for a particular member of your family.

First steps in family history    Caribbean    Irish    Jewish    South Asian

▶ **SEE ALSO:** Jewish Genealogy Society of Great Britain at www.jgsgb.org.uk.

▶ **SEE ALSO:** The National Archives site explores the presence of Asian and African peoples in the UK – see www.nationalarchives.gov.uk/pathways/blackhistory.

# Learn about emigration patterns

There is no one central set of records documenting people who left the UK. Many of the best records are found in the archives of destination countries. Fortunately for the family historian, many of these records (mostly in the form of passenger lists) are available online. If you lose track of a relative, it could be that they emigrated from the UK during the following periods:

- Southern Australia: from 1847 to 1886 many British subjects from the UK travelled under an assisted immigration programme.
- Australia: from 1787 to 1868 more than 160,000 convicts were transported to Australia from the UK.
- Canada: from 1815 to 1850 upwards of 650,000 people left the UK to settle in Canada.
- New Zealand: the British began settling in New Zealand from 1840 onwards.

 **DID YOU KNOW?**
Between 1890 and 1941 more than 200,000 people annually migrated to Australia, Canada and the US.

 **ALERT:** You will need information about your ancestors' ports of arrival and departure at a minimum. Having the name of the ship and reason for emigration will also help your search.

▶ **SEE ALSO:** www.theshipslist.com is a useful resource site about UK passengers who left for Australia, Canada and the United States.

# Search emigration records on ancestorsonboard

This site is a great source of information about your relative who left the UK for another country. There is a searchable database of passenger lists records from 1890 to 1960 for people who left for locations including the US, Australia, Canada, New Zealand and South Africa. If you registered and bought credits on the 1911census site or the findmypast site, you can use your credits to search here.

**1** Go to www.ancestorsonboard.com.

**2** Enter the details for your relative.

**3** Select a destination country and port if you know it and click Search.

**ALERT:** After you click Search you will be taken to the findmypast.co.uk website.

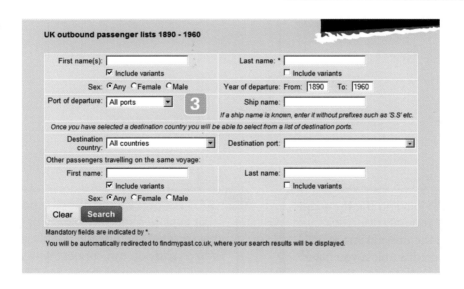

**4** Click View transcript.

## passenger transcript details

Name: **Mrs WALKER**
Date of departure: **28 April 1922**
Port of departure: **Southampton**
Passenger destination port: **Cape, South Africa**
Passenger destination: **Cape, South Africa**
Date of Birth: **1895 (calculated from age)**
Age: **27**
Marital status: **Married**
Sex: **Female**
Occupation:
Passenger recorded on: **Page 2 of 8**

PRINTER FRIENDLY VERSION

VIEW ORIGINAL IMAGE

The following people with the same last name travelled on this voyage: -

| Mr N L WALKER | Page 2 of 8 | View transcript |
| Mr R Mcneill WALKER | Page 5 of 8 | View transcript |

**4**

Ship: **ARMADALE CASTLE**
Official Number: **118350**
Master's name: **H Strong**
Steamship Line: **Union-Castle Mail Steamship Coy Ltd**
Where bound: **South Africa**
Square feet: **6670**
Registered tonnage: **12973**
Passengers on voyage: **199**

REPORT TRANSCRIPTION CHANGE

**ALERT:** Viewing the transcript will cost you only five credits. Viewing the original image will cost 30 credits unless you have a subscription to view these records.

**SEE ALSO:** Joining message boards that explore a specific country or ethnic background can provide useful clues for your search and you can connect with others who share a common heritage. See Chapter 9 for information on how to do this.

**SEE ALSO:** There are also some records on the site for individuals who left for different parts of Asia, South America, the Caribbean and West Africa.

**HOT TIP:** The passenger lists on this site include not only emigrants but also individuals who left for business or tourism.

# Search ellisisland.org

If one or more of your ancestors immigrated to the United States from 1890 to 1924, this site may contain a record of their arrival.

**1** Go to http://ellisisland.org.

**2** Enter the details for your relative and click Search.

**3** Click on the image link you want to view (passenger record, ship manifest, ship image).

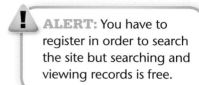

**ALERT:** You have to register in order to search the site but searching and viewing records is free.

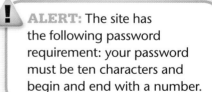

| Exact Matches (419) | | | | | | |
|---|---|---|---|---|---|---|
| Name of Passenger | Residence | Arrived | Age on Arrival | Passenger Record | Ship Manifest | Ship Image |
| 1. J. Burke | | 1894 | 16 | View | View | View |
| 2. J. Burke | | 1922 | 37 | View | View | View |
| 3. J. Burke | | 1922 | 46 | View | View | View |
| 4. J. J. Burke | | 1920 | 41 | View | View | View |
| 5. J. P. Burke | | 1920 | 36 | View | View | View |
| 6. J. W. Burke | | 1910 | 25 | View | View | View |
| 7. J.J. Burke | | 1920 | 39 | View | View | View |
| 8. Jack Burke | | 1911 | 30 | View | View | View |
| 9. Jacob Burke | London | 1906 | 21 | View | View | View |
| 10. James Burke | | 1895 | 13 | View | View | View |
| 11. James Burke | | 1903 | 18 | View | View | View |
| 12. James Burke | | 1906 | 20 | View | View | View |
| 13. James Burke | | 1908 | 24 | View | View | View |
| 14. James Burke | | 1912 | 28 | View | View | View |
| 15. James Burke | | 1905 | 29 | View | View | View |
| 16. James Burke | | 1911 | 30 | View | View | View |
| 17. James Burke | | 1913 | 34 | View | View | View |
| 18. James Burke | | 1911 | 35 | View | View | View |
| 19. James Burke | | 1917 | 35 | View | View | View |
| 20. James Burke | | 1919 | 36 | View | View | View |
| 21. James Burke | | 1922 | 38 | View | View | View |

**4** Click Yes I am new to this site and enter your details in the registration pages.

**5** Click Continue.

**6** Click View on the result you are interested in.

**ALERT:** The site has the following password requirement: your password must be ten characters and begin and end with a number.

PASSENGER RECORD

American Family Immigration History Center® at Ellis Island

First Name: Jacob
Last Name: Burke
Ethnicity: Russian, Hebrew
Last Place of Residence: London
Date of Arrival: Nov 05, 1906
Age at Arrival: 21y   Gender: M   Marital Status: S
Ship of Travel: Saint Paul
Port of Departure: Southampton
Manifest Line Number: 0016

**HOT TIP:** Write down all user names and passwords in a safe location as you register to use each new site.

**HOT TIP:** You can purchase copies of the individual passenger record or the ship's manifest on this site.

# Explore Library and Archives Canada

These archives have recently published records of passenger lists from 1865 to 1922. If your ancestor left the UK for Canada during this period, spend time searching this site. At present, you cannot search by individual name so you will need some information about their dates and ports of departure or arrival. One major advantage of this site is that you can search and view original images for free.

**1** Go to www.collectionscanada.gc.ca/databases/passenger/001045-130-e.html.

**2** Enter the details you know and click Submit.

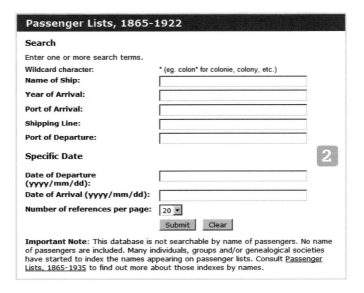

**Passenger Lists, 1865-1922**

**Search**

Enter one or more search terms.

Wildcard character:     * (eg. colon* for colonie, colony, etc.)

Name of Ship:

Year of Arrival:

Port of Arrival:

Shipping Line:

Port of Departure:

**Specific Date**

Date of Departure (yyyy/mm/dd):

Date of Arrival (yyyy/mm/dd):

Number of references per page:   20

Submit   Clear

**Important Note**: This database is not searchable by name of passengers. No name of passengers are included. Many individuals, groups and/or genealogical societies have started to index the names appearing on passenger lists. Consult Passenger Lists, 1865-1935 to find out more about those indexes by names.

---

**! ALERT:** There is usually more than one original image to view. Click the arrows next to the words Page Navigation to view subsequent records.

Page Navigation (3 pages): **1** ≥ >>

**? DID YOU KNOW?**

This database contains passenger lists for the following ports: Quebec, Halifax, Saint John, North Sydney, Vancouver, Victoria, New York and the Eastern American coast.

3 Scan the results and click on a ship link you want to view.

4 Click View Image to see a scan of the original image.

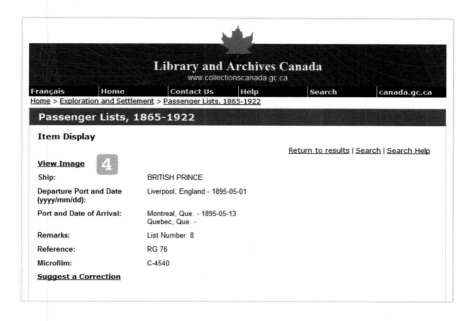

Library and Archives Canada
www.collectionscanada.gc.ca

| Français | Home | Contact Us | Help | Search | canada.gc.ca |

Home > Exploration and Settlement > Passenger Lists, 1865-1922

**Passenger Lists, 1865-1922**

**Item Display**

Return to results | Search | Search Help

**View Image** 4

| Ship: | BRITISH PRINCE |
| Departure Port and Date (yyyy/mm/dd): | Liverpool, England - 1895-05-01 |
| Port and Date of Arrival: | Montreal, Que. - 1895-05-13<br>Quebec, Que. - |
| Remarks: | List Number: 8 |
| Reference: | RG 76 |
| Microfilm: | C-4540 |

**Suggest a Correction**

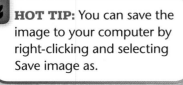

**HOT TIP:** You can save the image to your computer by right-clicking and selecting Save image as.

# Look at FamilySearch for bounty immigrant records to Australia

If your ancestor migrated to Australia between 1828 and 1842, it is worth searching the records on this site. The records in this collection consist of immigrants who participated in something called the bounty immigrant programme sponsored by the Australian government. Bounty immigrants were those with desirable skills who were given incentives to immigrate.

1 Go to www.familysearch.org.

2 Scroll down and click the link for Australia and New Zealand.

3 Click Index to Bounty Immigrants Arriving in N.S.W.

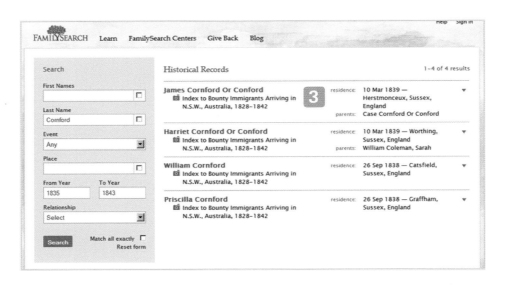

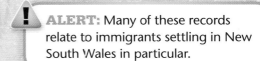

**DID YOU KNOW?**
Bounty immigrants were reimbursed for all or part of the cost of their journey after working for their colonist sponsor for a set period of time after their arrival.

**ALERT:** Many of these records relate to immigrants settling in New South Wales in particular.

4 Enter your relative's details and click Search.

5 Click on a historical record and view or save the record.

## Index to Bounty Immigrants Arriving in N.S.W., Australia, 1828-1842 for James Cornford Or Conford

« Back to search results

| | |
|---|---|
| principal's name: | **James Cornford Or Conford** |
| estimated birth year: | 1813 |
| age in years: | 26 |
| native place of principal: | Herstmonceux, Sussex, England |
| father's name: | Case Cornford Or Conford |
| mother's name: | |
| spouse's name: | Harriet Cornford Or Conford |
| native place of spouse: | Worthing, Sussex, England |
| spouse's father's name: | William Coleman |
| spouse's mother's name: | Sarah |
| ship: | Susan |
| date of arrival: | 10 Mar 1839 |
| volume: | 25 |
| gs number: | 416871 |
| dgs number: | 4117080 |
| image number: | 03251 |

■ View image

5

↓ Save image

**? DID YOU KNOW?**

The first wave of immigrants travelling with this programme were from the UK and Ireland, but later individuals from Europe followed suit.

# Explore FamilySearch for migrants to New Zealand

From 1840 to 1907, most of the people arriving in New Zealand were from the UK and Ireland. This site contains an excellent collection of searchable passenger records.

1 Go to www.familysearch.org.

2 Scroll down and click the link for Australia and New Zealand.

3 Click New Zealand, Immigration Passenger lists, 1855–1973.

4 Enter the details for your relative and click Search.

5 Click on the link for your relative and click View image (if there is one linked).

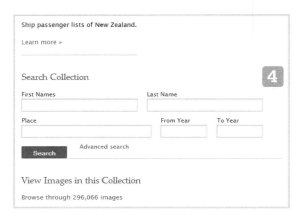

**HOT TIP:** Use the zoom function in the lower right corner to see more detail of the image.

**DID YOU KNOW?**
Many of the records for those travelling under the assisted immigration programme contain a wealth of information, including occupation and details of family members.

# Search for assisted immigrants to Australia

Many British subjects emigrated under an assisted programme either because of their skill set or as an alternative to receiving poor relief. Between 1839 and 1871 many of these immigrants arrived in Victoria, Australia. The Public Record Office of Victoria has an index of many of these travellers that you can search for free.

**1** Go to www.prov.vic.gov.au/indexes/index_search.asp?searchid=24.

**2** Enter the details for your relative and click Search.

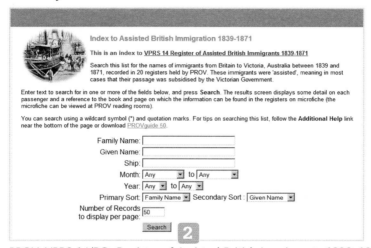

**Index to Assisted British Immigration 1839-1871**

This is an index to **VPRS 14 Register of Assisted British Immigrants 1839-1871**

Search this list for the names of immigrants from Britain to Victoria, Australia between 1839 and 1871, recorded in 20 registers held by PROV. These immigrants were 'assisted', meaning in most cases that their passage was subsidised by the Victorian Government.

Enter text to search for in one or more of the fields below, and press Search. The results screen displays some detail on each passenger and a reference to the book and page on which the information can be found in the registers on microfiche (the microfiche can be viewed at PROV reading rooms).

You can search using a wildcard symbol (*) and quotation marks. For tips on searching this list, follow the **Additional Help** link near the bottom of the page or download PROVguide 50.

Family Name: ☐
Given Name: ☐
Ship: ☐
Month: Any ▾ to Any ▾
Year: Any ▾ to Any ▾
Primary Sort: Family Name ▾ Secondary Sort : Given Name ▾
Number of Records to display per page: 50

Search

PROV, VPRS 14/PO: Register of Assisted British Immigrants 1839–1871

**3** Review the index or click Return to Search page to revise your search.

| Family Name ▵ | Given Name ▵ | Age ▵ | Month ▵ | Year ▵ | Ship ▵ | Book | Page |
|---|---|---|---|---|---|---|---|
| TAYLOR | ALICE | 18 | JUL | 1854 | MARIA HAY | 10 | 297 |
| TAYLOR | ALICE | 19 | DEC | 1863 | GRESHAM | 13A | 266 |
| TAYLOR | ALICE | 24 | JUL | 1867 | ATALANTA | 14A | 153 |
| TAYLOR | ALICE | 19 | DEC | 1863 | GRESHAM | 14 | 277 |
| TAYLOR | ALICE | 24 | JUL | 1867 | ATALANTA | 14 | 364 |

PROV, VPRS 14/PO, Book numbers 10, 13A, 14A and 14: Search results from the index to Assisted British Immigrants 1839–1871

**ALERT:** The book and page information at the end of the index is a reference to the microfilm of the records, held only at the record office of Victoria.

**SEE ALSO:** Some of these records are available to search on Ancestry.co.uk if you have a global membership type. See Chapter 7 for more information.

# Explore convict transport registers to Australia

You can find details for your more colourful ancestors in a number of online sources. One great site to try is convictrecords.com.au, which contains a good collection of records for the British convict transportation register for convicts transported to Australia from 1787 to 1867. You can browse and search for free.

1 Go to www.convictrecords.com.au.

2 Enter the first and last name of your relative if you know them.

3 Click Search.

4 If you do not find information for your relative, you can browse the records by surname, year and ship.

 **DID YOU KNOW?**
This collection consists mostly of individuals convicted in England, Wales and Scotland, with only a few records for Irish convicts.

 **SEE ALSO:** Click advanced search options if you have details about the year of transportation or the name of the ship your relative was on.

▶ **SEE ALSO:** www.blacksheepancestors.com/uk has links to information and resources related to convict transportation to Australia as well as information about prison records in the UK.

# 7 Join ancestry.co.uk

# Introduction

Using the pay-as-you-go option can become less economical the further you get in your family research. At this point you may want to consider a subscription to the largest global online genealogy site. In addition to the BMD, census and immigration records which you have already explored, the site contains millions of other records as well as an excellent online family tree program.

# Consider joining ancestry.co.uk

The easy-to-navigate site, wealth of records and family tree tool have made Ancestry the most popular genealogy site worldwide. The website below is dedicated to UK family history (as opposed to ancestry.com) and all of the records and resources are designed to meet the needs of researchers in the UK. With an ancestry subscription you can do the following:

- Sign up for a 14-day free trial.
- Attach documents from the site to your online family tree.
- Search the large collection of military and immigration records.
- Browse the criminal registers, probate records and wills.
- Upgrade to a worldwide membership.

**ALERT:** Worldwide membership gives you access to Australian and US immigration records as well as a variety of Irish historical records.

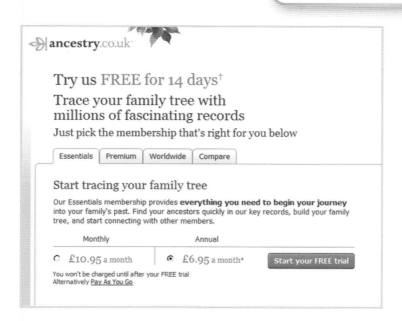

 **HOT TIP:** The free trial is based on the type of subscription you are interested in.

 **ALERT:** If you continue to use pay-as-you-go credits, they must be used within 14 days or you will lose them.

# Choose a subscription type

You can start with a 14-day free trial based on the subscription type you are interested in. Ancestry offers three types of subscription based on the number of records you have access to view. One way to see whether a subscription type would be of interest to you is to sign up for the free trial.

**1** Go to www.ancestry.co.uk.

**2** Click Sign up for a 14-day free trial.

**3** Click the membership type tabs or click Compare.

**4** Select Monthly or Annual once you choose a membership.

**5** Click Start Your 14-Day Free Trial.

**6** Enter your details, tick the relevant boxes and click Continue.

**7** Continue through the registration fields to subscribe.

 **HOT TIP:** Read and tick or untick the boxes in the registration field before you click Continue.

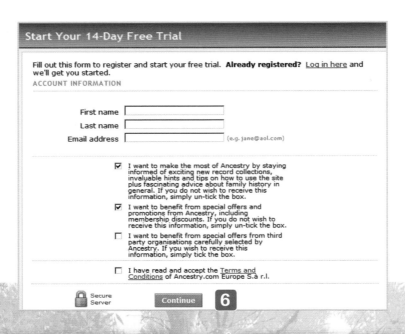

**Start Your 14-Day Free Trial**

Fill out this form to register and start your free trial. **Already registered?** Log in here and we'll get you started.

ACCOUNT INFORMATION

First name [ ]
Last name [ ]
Email address [ ]   (e.g. jane@aol.com)

☑ I want to make the most of Ancestry by staying informed of exciting new record collections, invaluable hints and tips on how to use the site plus fascinating advice about family history in general. If you do not wish to receive this information, simply un-tick the box.

☑ I want to benefit from special offers and promotions from Ancestry, including membership discounts. If you do not wish to receive this information, simply un-tick the box.

☐ I want to benefit from special offers from third party organisations carefully selected by Ancestry. If you wish to receive this information, simply tick the box.

☐ I have read and accept the Terms and Conditions of Ancestry.com Europe S.à r.l.

🔒 Secure Server   [ Continue ]   **6**

⚠ **ALERT:** You will need to provide a credit card while registering for your free trial.

⚠ **ALERT:** You must cancel your subscription *before* the end of the 14-day trial period (if you choose not to subscribe) or your card will be charged.

# Start a family tree

Ancestry has a tool that allows you to create a digital version of your family tree. The tree on this site is more than a visual reference of your research; as you add to it, the site will automatically search the records for information about your relatives. The first step is entering the details you know into the tree.

**1** Put your cursor on Family Trees.

**2** Select Start a new tree.

**3** Select I am starting with myself and enter your details.

**4** Enter the details for your father, your mother and click Continue.

**5** Name your family tree and click Done.

**6** Click Skip for now (when offered to send the tree to others).

**? DID YOU KNOW?**
You can make more than one tree on this site and save them under different file names.

**! ALERT:** Ticking Allow others to view your tree lets other members view the names and details in your tree.

# Edit your tree settings

One benefit of using a large subscription site is being able to share information with others who may share ancestors with you. You may want to consider maintaining a public tree with the hope that you can benefit from others' research. Alternatively, if you feel strongly that you want to keep your research private, you need to edit the settings to do this (if you did not do so when you registered).

**1** Click on the Family Trees menu and select a tree.

**2** While in your tree, point your cursor to the Tree pages link.

**3** Select Tree Settings.

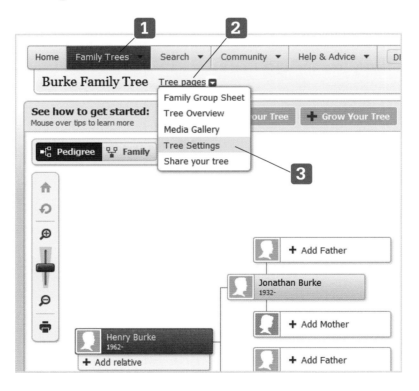

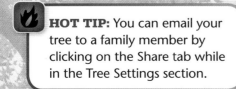

**HOT TIP:** You can email your tree to a family member by clicking on the Share tab while in the Tree Settings section.

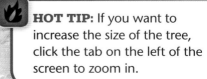

**HOT TIP:** If you want to increase the size of the tree, click the tab on the left of the screen to zoom in.

4 Click Privacy Settings.

5 Select either the Public or Private Tree option.

6 Click Save Changes.

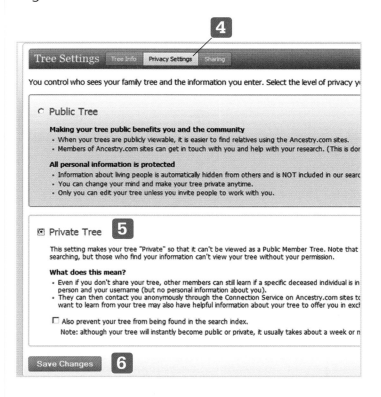

**Tree Settings** Tree Info | Privacy Settings | Sharing

You control who sees your family tree and the information you enter. Select the level of privacy y⟨

○ **Public Tree**

**Making your tree public benefits you and the community**
- When your trees are publicly viewable, it is easier to find relatives using the Ancestry.com sites.
- Members of Ancestry.com sites can get in touch with you and help with your research. (This is dor⟨

**All personal information is protected**
- Information about living people is automatically hidden from others and is NOT included in our searc⟨
- You can change your mind and make your tree private anytime.
- Only you can edit your tree unless you invite people to work with you.

◉ **Private Tree**

This setting makes your tree "Private" so that it can't be viewed as a Public Member Tree. Note that searching, but those who find your information can't view your tree without your permission.

**What does this mean?**
- Even if you don't share your tree, other members can still learn if a specific deceased individual is in person and your username (but no personal information about you).
- They can then contact you anonymously through the Connection Service on Ancestry.com sites to want to learn from your tree may also have helpful information about your tree to offer you in exc⟨

☐ Also prevent your tree from being found in the search index.
   Note: although your tree will instantly become public or private, it usually takes about a week or n⟨

**Save Changes**

---

## WHAT DOES THIS MEAN?

**Pedigree** view only shows details for you, your parents, grandparents, etc. **Family** view shows one nuclear family.

# Add to your tree

If you have found details for other relatives during your research up to this point, add them to your tree now. You can also add photographs to the site if you have them.

**1** Click the Family Trees menu and select your tree.

**2** Point the cursor to a person in the tree until a box appears.

**3** Click Add relative and select a relative to enter (father, mother, spouse or child).

**4** Enter the details for the person and click Save.

**5** Repeat this process for each individual for whom you have details.

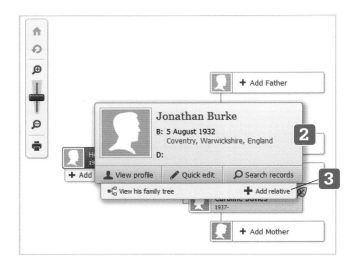

**! ALERT:** If you add children to an individual's record, they will not show up while you are in Pedigree view. Click the family group sheet in your tree to view details of your relative's children.

**? DID YOU KNOW?**
You can add a photograph by clicking Upload photos while in an individual ancestor's Profile view.

# Search for records from your tree

You can focus on one individual in your tree and search the records for that individual while in your tree. This saves you the trouble of entering all their dates and information each time you search. While in the tree view:

**1** Point your cursor to an individual in your tree.

**2** Click Search records.

**3** Review the results and click a relevant link.

**4** If you do not get the results you want:

- Click a category to search (census, immigration, etc.).
- Click Edit Search to change the details of the search.

**HOT TIP:** If you do not find information for your relative, change your search criteria by using alternative spellings and dates.

# Attach records to your tree

Once you find a record that you believe belongs to a person in your tree, you can attach that record to their profile within your tree. Always review the information in the record carefully and compare it with what you know about your relative before deciding it belongs to them.

**1** Find a record you want to attach.

**2** Click View original image.

**3** Click the orange Save tab.

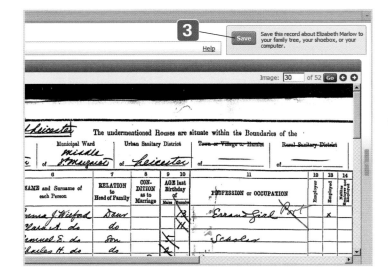

**4** Select Attach this record to [your relative].

**5** Click Continue.

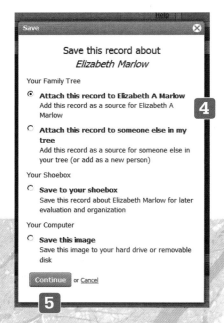

**! ALERT:** The search engine won't find all records relevant to your ancestor; you will still need to search through the collections yourself for information.

**HOT TIP:** Select Save to your shoebox if you are not certain the record belongs to your relative. You can review the record again at a later point by returning to your shoebox on the home page.

# Review record hints

When you notice a leaf symbol next to one of your relatives in your tree, it means that the search engine has a possible record match for your relative. The record hint can be either from the collections (BMD, Census, etc.) or from another member's family tree.

**1** Point your cursor at the individual with a leaf.

**2** Click Ancestry hint.

**3** Click Review hint.

**4** Compare the hint with the data from your tree.

**5** Click Save to your tree or Cancel if it is not a match.

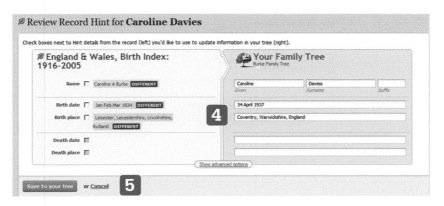

**ALERT:** Read the details carefully before saving the record hint to your tree. The hints are merely possible matches for your relative – only you can discern whether or not the record belongs to your relative.

**DID YOU KNOW?** You can click on another member's tree when it comes up as a records hint to check for additional details about your shared ancestry.

# Search the collections

If you did not buy credits to view BMD, census and immigration records in previous chapters, you can search those records now. First you will need to check that you have the subscription type that allows you to search all of these collections.

**1** Point your cursor at the Search tab.

**2** Select a record collection that you want to search.

**3** Enter the details for your relative and click Search.

**4** Review the results and view original image.

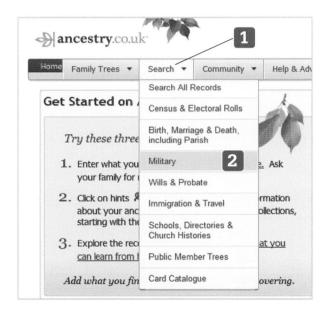

**? DID YOU KNOW?**

The military collection on ancestry contains army service records and pension records for the First and Second World Wars.

**? DID YOU KNOW?**

There is also an index of wills and probate records, city and county directories as well as telephone and professional directories.

# Browse the message boards

Ancestry has a growing number of message boards where you can view others member's research queries or post your own questions. Participating in online discussion groups is explored more thoroughly in Chapter 9.

**1** Point your cursor at the Community tab.

**2** Select Message Boards.

**3** Scroll down to view category groups.

**4** Click a category folder and click again until you find a group to browse.

**5** Click a message to view it.

**6** View the replies beneath the message by clicking on them.

📂 **United Kingdom and Ireland**
⭐ Add Category to Favourites (See All)

UNITED KINGDOM AND IRELAND CATEGORIES

| Category |
| --- |
| 📂 British Overseas Territories |
| 📂 Channel Islands |
| 📂 England |
| 📂 Ireland |
| 📂 Isle of Man |
| 📂 Scotland |
| 📂 Wales |

**3**

UNITED KINGDOM AND IRELAND BOARDS

| Board | Threads | Messages |
| --- | --- | --- |
| 🗄 General | 1945 | 8479 |
| 🗄 Historical British Empire | 19 | 98 |

🗄 **General**
📝 Begin New Thread                    Threads: 4466 - Messages: 15804
📶 Subscribe to RSS

| Thread | Author | Replies | Last Post |
| --- | --- | --- | --- |
| marriages in scotland 1892 and 1889 | LindaClark195... | 2 | 5 Apr 2011 |
| Linen Merchants Trade Orginization in Scotland | RCBoss99 | 2 | 30 Mar 2011 |
| marriages in scotland in 1889 and 1892 | LindaClark195... | 3 | 18 Mar 2011 |
| Marriage in Scotland in 1800s | kelvinbell1 | 4 | 14 Mar 2011 |
| General question about extracted probate records | mtngal67 | 7 | 4 Mar 2011 |
| where is Dundee? | Robert Hay-Hendry | 3 | 25 Feb 2011 |
| GeoGenealogy's Gazetteer of Scotland | howardmathies... | 0 | 24 Jan 2011 |
| Widows - Do they go back to using their maiden names in Scotland? | GretchenGenea... | 6 | 3 Jan 2011 |
| When did Scotland stop writing illegitimate on the birth lines? | pepsidogy | 1 | 7 Dec 2010 |
| Help with Scottish legal terms 1800s | craig_C_Colli... | 1 | 3 Dec 2010 |

**5**

Results per page 10 ▾                    Viewing 1 - 10 of 4466 | Next >>

Posts to this board are copied to the "SCOTLAND-L" RootsWeb.com mailing list.

**❓ DID YOU KNOW?**
You can search for a specific keyword (i.e. city, village, surname) by entering the term into the first field on the message board page.

**🔥 HOT TIP:** You can also search for a board topic by entering a topic yourself into the second field on the message board page.

# Print ancestry forms

It is tremendously helpful as you find more information for your relatives to have a written copy of your work to keep yourself on track. When you are presented with a possible ancestry record match, having the family details before you will help you decide whether or not the record belongs to your relative.

**1** Point your cursor to the Help & Advice tab.

**2** Select Family history advice.

**3** Click Useful charts and forms.

**4** Click Family history charts and forms.

**5** Click Download Form.

**6** Print the form or save it to your computer.

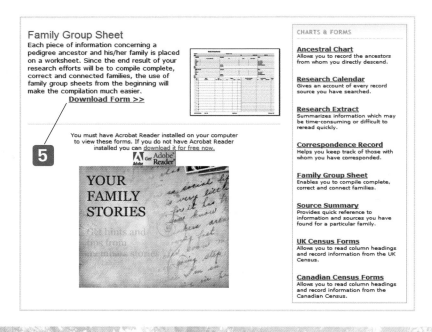

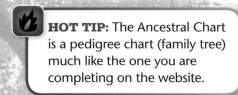

**HOT TIP:** The Ancestral Chart is a pedigree chart (family tree) much like the one you are completing on the website.

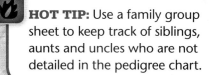

**HOT TIP:** Use a family group sheet to keep track of siblings, aunts and uncles who are not detailed in the pedigree chart.

# 8 Join findmypast.co.uk

# Introduction

This easy-to-use family history website has a good collection of records and flexible subscription and pay-as-you-go options for the beginner. Saving and printing original images is straightforward and you can create an online family tree.

# Consider joining findmypast.co.uk

This website is dedicated exclusively to researching family history in the UK. Presently, it is the only genealogy site to have the 1911 census records and it has many other unique features that are worth considering. With findmypast.co.uk you can:

- Buy credits that can be used for up to a year.
- Choose a 6- or 12-month subscription.
- Search for emigrants who left the UK.
- Search census records by address as well as name.
- Match marriage registry information for both spouses.
- Explore overseas and military records.

**ALERT:** The 14-day trial will provide you with a foundation membership for 14 days, which allows you to search BMDs and census records but not specialist records.

**SEE ALSO:** If you had relatives in London from the 16th to the 18th century, you can search for them in the fascinating Boyd's Inhabitants of London and Boyd's Family Units on this site.

# Start a trial subscription

findmypast.co.uk allows you to try the site before you decide to subscribe. The trial membership gives you a foundation subscription for 14 days. This type of membership allows you to search and view original images of BMDs and census records. It will not allow you to search the military, parish, migration and the other specialist records on the site.

1. Go to www.findmypast.co.uk.

2. Click Start a 14 day free trial.

3. Click the green Start your free trial tab.

4. In the registration fields, enter your details and click Register.

5. Enter your card details and click Submit.

6. Click Start your free trial.

 **ALERT:** You will need to leave your credit card details to start your 14-day trial.

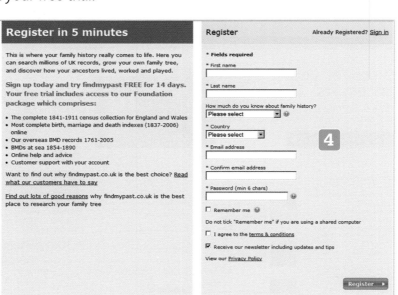

Register in 5 minutes

This is where your family history really comes to life. Here you can search millions of UK records, grow your own family tree, and discover how your ancestors lived, worked and played.

**Sign up today and try findmypast FREE for 14 days. Your free trial includes access to our Foundation package which comprises:**

- The complete 1841-1911 census collection for England and Wales
- Most complete birth, marriage and death indexes (1837-2006) online
- Our overseas BMD records 1761-2005
- BMDs at sea 1854-1890
- Online help and advice
- Customer support with your account

Want to find out why findmypast.co.uk is the best choice? Read what our customers have to say

Find out lots of good reasons why findmypast.co.uk is the best place to research your family tree

Register        Already Registered? Sign in

* Fields required
* First name
* Last name
How much do you know about family history?
Please select
* Country
Please select
* Email address
* Confirm email address
* Password (min 6 chars)
☐ Remember me
Do not tick "Remember me" if you are using a shared computer
☐ I agree to the terms & conditions
☑ Receive our newsletter including updates and tips
View our Privacy Policy

Register ►

**ALERT:** You must cancel your subscription a day *prior* to the end of your 14-day trial or your card will be charged. Go to My account on the website's main page to do so.

**HOT TIP:** You can continue to use a pay-as-you-go account for up to a year on this site. This option gives you access to all of the records (specialist as well as BMD, census and parish records).

# Create a tree on Family Tree Explorer

As you find more details of your family history, you can add them to a digital family tree through this site. The Family Tree Explorer is an easy-to-use, visually interesting way to organise your work online.

**1** Click the Family Trees tab at the top of the page.

**2** Click Create your family tree (a new window will open).

**3** Enter details for you and your parents and click Next after each step.

**4** At step 4, enter your email address and password.

**5** Tick I Agree to Terms and Conditions and click Next.

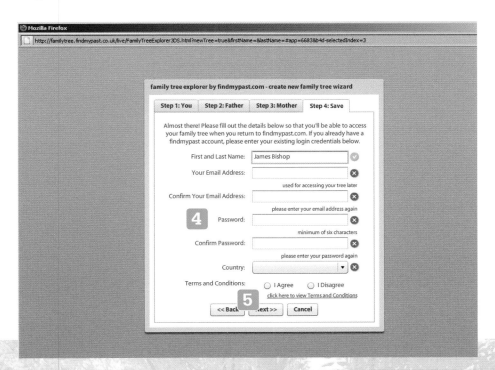

**ALERT:** The Family Tree Explorer is an online application that you do not have to download to your computer – the website will store all of your information for you.

**HOT TIP:** You can attach saved documents to an individual in your tree by clicking on that person and selecting Media in the box on the right.

6 Select a privacy setting and click Next.

7 Click View Tree.

130

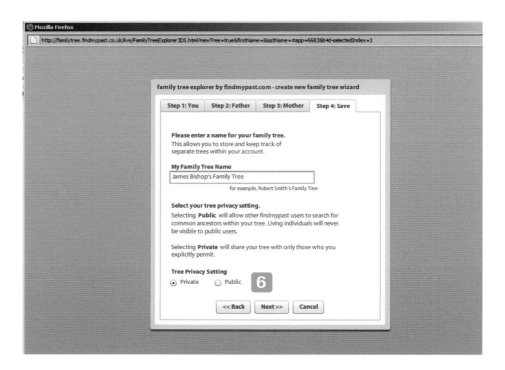

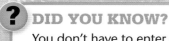 **DID YOU KNOW?**

You don't have to enter every detail for relatives in your tree when you create a tree, you will be able to go back and edit the tree later.

# Add to your family tree

Once you have created a tree you can add to or edit the information as you find new records and information for your ancestors. Check that you are signed into your account before you click on the Family Trees section of the website.

**1** Click Family Trees at the top of the page.

**2** Click Create or View a tree.

**3** Move your cursor to the person you want to add to.

**4** Click on a plus arrow.

> **ALERT:** You can further edit the details of a person in the tree by clicking on that person and entering details into the box on the right.

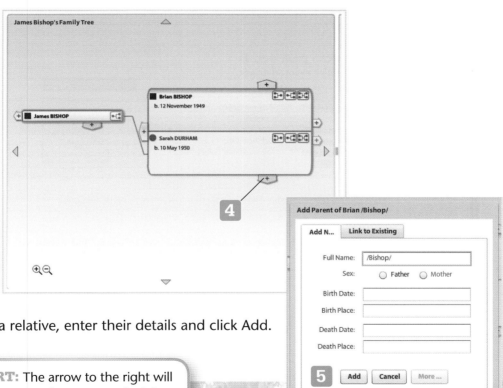

**5** Select a relative, enter their details and click Add.

> **ALERT:** The arrow to the right will add a parent; the arrow to the left will add a child.

> **HOT TIP:** You can print your completed tree by clicking File and then selecting Print.

> **HOT TIP:** Once your tree gets larger, click on the arrow keys around the edges of the screen to view a different section of the tree.

# Use the MarriageFinder™

One challenge of searching for marriage registry information is finding details of the person's spouse. Before 1912, a spouse's last name was not listed on marriage indexes. On this site, the records have been cross referenced and the search engine displays a possible match for your relative.

1 Click Births, Marriages & Deaths at the top of the page.

2 Scroll to the Marriages section and click Search.

3 Enter the details for your relative, select a county and click Search.

4 Review the results and click View record for your relative.

5 Write down the reference information or save the document.

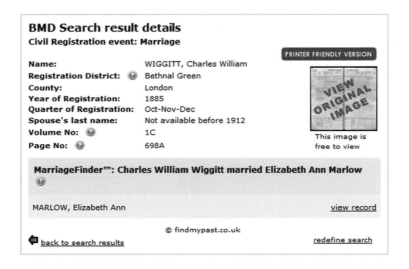

**BMD Search result details**
**Civil Registration event: Marriage**

PRINTER FRIENDLY VERSION

| | |
|---|---|
| **Name:** | WIGGITT, Charles William |
| **Registration District:** | Bethnal Green |
| **County:** | London |
| **Year of Registration:** | 1885 |
| **Quarter of Registration:** | Oct-Nov-Dec |
| **Spouse's last name:** | Not available before 1912 |
| **Volume No:** | 1C |
| **Page No:** | 698A |

VIEW ORIGINAL IMAGE

This image is free to view

**MarriageFinder™: Charles William Wiggitt married Elizabeth Ann Marlow**

MARLOW, Elizabeth Ann                                      view record

© findmypast.co.uk

⬅ back to search results                                    redefine search

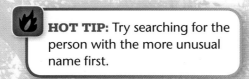

**HOT TIP:** Try searching for the person with the more unusual name first.

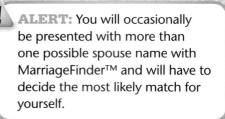

**ALERT:** You will occasionally be presented with more than one possible spouse name with MarriageFinder™ and will have to decide the most likely match for yourself.

# Search census records by address

If you have an address for one of your relatives from another source (birth certificate, marriage certificate, correspondence, etc.) you can search for the census records for them. All you need is the street name and the county they lived in.

1 Click the Census tab at the top of the page.

2 Select a census year and click Search by address.

3 Enter the street name, select the county and click Search.

**1911 address search**

| basic search | advanced search | search tips |
|---|---|---|

Street name:

Ronald St.

**3**

Residential place:

County:

London

Sort results by:

Street A - Z

Wildcard search (e.g. HI*) available in all boxes above, apart from the drop-down menus. You must also enter a Residential Place if you use the wildcard search.

CLEAR   SEARCH

4 Click VIEW next to a street number.

**1911 census - street details**

**Search criteria used:**
County: London        Street name: Ronald St.
Residential Place:
**Results:**
Your search has returned total 42 results.

| Schedule | House ▼ | Street | Civil Parish | Registration District | County | View Address Transcript |
|---|---|---|---|---|---|---|
| 358 | 2 | Ronald St | Ratcliff | Stepney | London | VIEW |
| 356 | 4 | Ronald St | Ratcliff | Stepney | London | VIEW |
| 357 | 4 | Ronald St | Ratcliff | Stepney | London | VIEW |
| 317 | 5 | Ronald St | Ratcliff | Stepney | London | VIEW |
| 318 | 5 | Ronald St | Ratcliff | Stepney | London | VIEW |
| 354 | 6 | Ronald St | Ratcliff | Stepney | London | VIEW |
| 355 | 6 | Ronald St | Ratcliff | Stepney | London | VIEW |
| 319 | 7 | Ronald St | Ratcliff | Stepney | London | VIEW |
| 320 | 7 | Ronald St | Ratcliff | Stepney | London | VIEW |
| 321 | 9 | Ronald St | Ratcliff | Stepney | London | VIEW |
| 322 | 9 | Ronald St | Ratcliff | Stepney | London | VIEW |
| 352 | 10 | Ronald St | Ratcliff | Stepney | London | VIEW |
| 353 | 10 | Ronald St | Ratcliff | Stepney | London | VIEW |
| 323 | 11 | Ronald St | Ratcliff | Stepney | London | VIEW |
| 324 | 11 | Ronald St | Ratcliff | Stepney | London | VIEW |
| 350 | 12 | Ronald St | Ratcliff | Stepney | London | VIEW |
| 351 | 12 | Ronald St | Ratcliff | Stepney | London | VIEW |
| 325 | 13 | Ronald St | Ratcliff | Stepney | London | VIEW |
| 326 | 13 | Ronald St | Ratcliff | Stepney | London | VIEW |
| 347 | 14 | Ronald St | Ratcliff | Stepney | London | VIEW |
| 348 | 14 | Ronald St | Ratcliff | Stepney | London | VIEW |
| 349 | 14 | Ronald St | Ratcliff | Stepney | London | VIEW ☆ |
| 327 | 15 | Ronald St | Ratcliff | Stepney | London | VIEW |

**4**

**ALERT:** Do not enter a street number in the search field as the database searches by street name only.

**SEE ALSO:** Make a note of your ancestors' addresses and occupations on the census. In Chapter 11 there are resources to help you research local and occupational history.

# Search military records

Most of the military records on the site relate to the First and Second World Wars. To search these records you must either have a full subscription or have purchased credits – you won't be able to view these with the 14-day trial subscription.

1 Click the Military tab at the top of the page.

2 Select a record set to search or select Search all.

3 Click Search.

4 Enter the details for your relative.

5 Enter a date range or select WW1 or WW2.

6 Click Search.

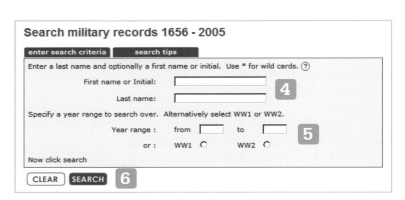

**Search military records 1656 - 2005**

| enter search criteria | search tips |

Enter a last name and optionally a first name or initial. Use * for wild cards. (?)

First name or Initial: [                    ]    **4**

Last name: [                    ]

Specify a year range to search over. Alternatively select WW1 or WW2.

Year range :    from [        ]    to [        ]    **5**

or :    WW1 ○    WW2 ○

Now click search

[ CLEAR ]  [ SEARCH ]    **6**

7 View the most likely results or redefine your search.

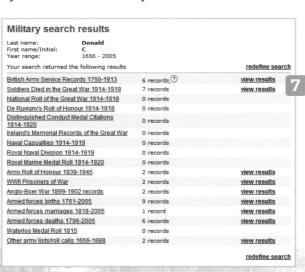

**Military search results**

Last name: **Donald**
First name/Initial: **C**
Year range: **1656 - 2005**

Your search returned the following results                    redefine search

| British Army Service Records 1760-1913 | 6 records (?) | view results | **7** |
| Soldiers Died in the Great War 1914-1919 | 7 records | view results |
| National Roll of the Great War 1914-1918 | 0 records |
| De Ruvigny's Roll of Honour 1914-1918 | 0 records |
| Distinguished Conduct Medal Citations 1914-1920 | 0 records |
| Ireland's Memorial Records of the Great War | 0 records |
| Naval Casualties 1914-1919 | 0 records |
| Royal Naval Division 1914-1919 | 0 records |
| Royal Marine Medal Roll 1914-1920 | 0 records |
| Army Roll of Honour 1939-1945 | 2 records | view results |
| WWII Prisoners of War | 2 records | view results |
| Anglo-Boer War 1899-1902 records | 2 records | view results |
| Armed forces births 1761-2005 | 9 records | view results |
| Armed forces marriages 1818-2005 | 1 record | view results |
| Armed forces deaths 1796-2005 | 6 records | view results |
| Waterloo Medal Roll 1815 | 0 records |
| Other army lists/roll calls 1656-1888 | 2 records | view results |

redefine search

 **HOT TIP:** You can view the armed forces' BMD records with your free trial subscription.

 **DID YOU KNOW?**

There are service records for the British army that span 1760–1913. If you had a relative in the army and find a record for them, you will often gain pages of valuable detail about them.

# Explore the specialist records

If you have a full subscription or have pay-as-you-go credits, spend time looking at the specialist records on this site. The records usually focus on a narrow area of history and will not be applicable to every family historian. However, if the records are relevant to your ancestor you may find excellent, often very detailed, clues about their lives. Some of the records include the following:

- Boyd's Inhabitants of London and Boyd's Family Units: contain names and information for more than 500,000 residents of London from the 16th to the 18th centuries.
- Teacher's Registration Council Registers 1914–1948: contain the details of 100,000 people (many women) who taught in England and Wales.
- Kelly's Handbook 1901: contains information about the titled, landed and official classes throughout the country for that year.
- The Medical Register 1913: contains the date of registration, address and list of qualifications for each doctor.

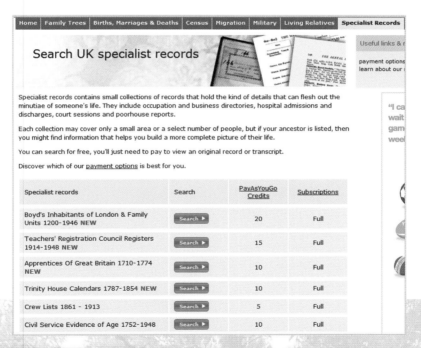

 **HOT TIP:** Click Search on the record set of interest and scroll down the page to read about the records and information they may contain.

# 9 Connect with others online

# Introduction

Online groups are a great way to learn more about family history and get help with your research. You can also find others who share your specific research interests (surname or geographic area) and even find cousins or other relatives you didn't know you had.

# Learn about mailing lists

Most lists focus on the common interests of members, such as geographical area, surname, occupation or even record type. They are discussion lists – members can send email messages to all other members at the same time and anyone can reply. Some lists have thousands of members and at least one or more moderator. On mailing lists you can:

- Learn about resources and research strategies from experienced family historians.
- Share your research with others.
- Ask for help when you are stuck with your search.

 **DID YOU KNOW?**
Group messages are sent directly to your email inbox. You generally get quick responses on a mailing list.

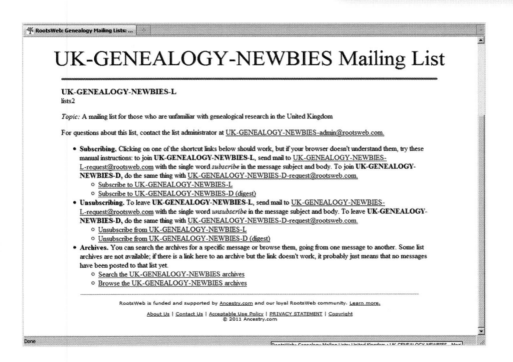

**WHAT DOES THIS MEAN?**
**Moderator:** the person who oversees the content of the list and reinforces the rules. This person usually has the power to delete posts that are not relevant to the group or posts that are potentially inflammatory.

# Understand web forums

A forum is a discussion group located on a specific webpage and the messages, referred to as posts, are all contained on that page. Your posts can be read by all members and, depending on the security of the site, others who visit the webpage. Like mailing lists, you can get answers to your family history questions and share your work with others. On family history forums you can:

- View the discussions you want without filling up your email box.
- View an ongoing discussion thread as it unfolds all on one page.
- Search old posts for information relevant to your research.
- Make contact with others who share your specific interests.

| Board name | Topics | Posts | Last post |
|---|---|---|---|
| **Beginners** | | | |
| **Beginners**<br>Everyone has to start somewhere, so why not start here. Post your genealogy questions on how to search your family history and post your local history questions here! Also, if you can think of things to help a budding local history or family history beginner, then please post your tips here!<br>See also **Help Pages: Guidelines to Posting** | 8970 | 73812 | **Today at 17:28:15**<br>in Re: Thomas Gayton & Jane<br>by patrish |
| **How to Use RootsChat**<br>If you have questions on how to use RootsChat, look in the **Help** Pages<br>For instance: **FAQs, Tips an Hints** or in the **Index to Help-Pages**<br>If you can't find the answers in the Help-Pages, then try here … | 999 | 8551 | **Yesterday at 11:28:38**<br>in Re: i get emails from th…<br>by NEILKE |
| ▼ **Old Photographs, Recognition, Handwriting Deciphering** | | | |
| **Photograph Restoration & Dating.**<br>Would you like a treasured photograph restored or dated ?<br>*Moderator: PrueM*<br>*Child Boards: Resources, Tips, Tutorials* | 20685 | 228619 | **Today at 17:25:42**<br>in Re: Please help Rhoda-co…<br>by originQuest |
| **Deciphering & Recognition Help**<br>Need help deciphering old handwriting on wills, certificates and other FH documents ?<br>Want to know where a place is on your old photos ?? Post your queries here .. | 3303 | 31787 | **Today at 14:12:34**<br>in Re: baptism record in Fr…<br>by Eidde |
| ▼ **General** | | | |
| **The Common Room**<br>Join in and discuss more general genealogy and local history things here. If you can't think of what category, country or county your message should come under, then perhaps you could put your message here!<br>*Child Boards: The Lighter Side, Totally Off Topic Bit* | 16772 | 193684 | **Today at 17:23:42**<br>in Re: Unusual Street Names<br>by KGarrad |
| **Technical Help**<br>Need some technical help with using your computer, or using the internet?<br>*Child Boards: FH Programs, Organisation, Presentation, Surname Interest Table, Webspace* | 4979 | 45356 | **Today at 15:43:26**<br>in Re: findmypast census 19…<br>by jim1 |
| **Useful Links**<br>Links to other local history or genealogy websites of interest | 519 | 1127 | Monday 25 April 11 08:16 BST (UK)<br>in Re: RootsChat Topics: X…<br>by Berlin-Bob |

**HOT TIP:** In general, you have to visit the webpage to see replies to your forum posts. Some sites allow you to select an email reply option so you can see the responses in your email box as well as online.

**ALERT:** Some forums require approval to join. You usually just send your personal details and information about your research interests.

# Learn about netiquette

In the absence of body language, tone of voice and the usual features of communication, online messages can be easily misinterpreted. In general, the use of humour, especially sarcasm, is discouraged as it can be misread. However, you can use emoticons to clarify your message if you want to convey humour or some other feeling.

Common rules of netiquette:

- Stick to the topic of the group.
- Make sure your subject line is clear.
- Don't use all capital letters – this is equivalent to shouting.
- Don't post multiple times on the same topic.

| | |
|---|---|
| :-) | Smiling, tongue-in-cheek |
| :-( | Sad |
| ;-) | Wink |
| :-0 | Surprise |
| :-< | Disappointed |
| :D | Big grin |

 **HOT TIP:** Concise posts stand the best chance of being read and responded to by others.

 **ALERT:** You should always ask permission before forwarding someone's email or post outside of the group.

# Understand internet jargon

While you are browsing through the online forums or when reading emails, you are likely to come across a series of acronyms and terms specific to the internet. There are also terms specific to family history that are good to know before you join an online community.

- Look ups – asking other members to look up an ancestor's record for you.
- PM – a private message between two members of the group that is not visible to others.
- Flame – a post that is viewed as angry or hostile by others.

FAQ = Frequently asked question

LOL = Laughing out loud

FYI = For your information

BTW = By the way

IMO = In my opinion

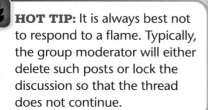
**HOT TIP:** It is always best not to respond to a flame. Typically, the group moderator will either delete such posts or lock the discussion so that the thread does not continue.

**ALERT:** You may violate copyright laws by asking for look ups of certain records. The forum or list you are part of will inform members of appropriate look up requests in the group rules.

# Find a mailing list on Rootsweb

Rootsweb was one of the earliest family history communities online. It boasts more than 30,000 international mailing lists and has countless members active online. The community is now hosted by Ancestry.com but you can join most of its mailing lists for free. However, some groups restrict access to members of a specific group, such as local history societies or surname groups.

**1** Go to http://lists.rootsweb.ancestry.com.

**2** Enter a term into the Find a mailing list field and click Find.

**3** Read the group's description or click more to check whether the group is of interest to you.

**4** Follow the instructions to register,

**5** Or note the subscription address and launch your mail program.

**6** Enter the address in your email, type *subscribe* in the subject line and send.

### Find a List Search

Viewing **1-25** of **501** matches from **32,097** mailing lists      1 2 3 4 5 6 7 8 9 10 11 12 13 14 15 16 17 18 19 20 21 | Next

| List Name | Description | Location | Surname | Category |
|---|---|---|---|---|
| LONDON | London | England, London / Greater London | | |
| ADAMS-ENG-LONDON | The ADAMS-ENG-LONDON mailing list is for the discussion and... more | | ADAMS | |
| LONDON-LIFE | A mailing list for the discussion and sharing... more | England | | |
| EOLFHS-MEMBERS | A mailing list for the members of the East of London... more | England, London / Greater London | | Genealogical Societies |
| 1-25TH-LONDON | The 1-25th London Cycle Regiment in WWI. Used... more | England | | Military: UK |
| LONDON-SURNAME | Discussing and sharing of information regarding... more | | LONDON | |
| FOSTER-RICHARD | The FOSTER-RICHARD mailing list is for the discussion... more | | FOSTER | |
| REDFIELD | primarily on surname REDFIELD, but also to include... more | | REDFIELD | |
| CTNEWLON | New London County, CT | USA, Connecticut, New London | | |
| TOLPUDDLE | The TOLPUDDLE mailing list is for the discussion... more | | TOLPUDDLE | |
| LONDON-COMPANYS | A mailing list for anyone with an interest in the... more | | | Occupations |
| ENGLAND-ROOTS | A mailing list for anyone with a genealogical interest... more | England | | |
| FOSTER-ENGLAND | Foster surname and variations in England. | | FOSTER | |
| ROGERS-JAMES-CT | This mailing list will be of interest to the descendants... more | | ROGERS | |
| GUYFAWKES | | England | | |
| OXFORDSHIRE | Oxfordshire | England, Oxfordshire / Oxon | | |
| Middlesex_County_UK | Middlesex County | England, Middlesex | | |
| DEVON | Devonshire | England, Devon or Devonshire | | |
| NORTHANTS | Northampton | England, Northampton | | |

**! ALERT:** If you click the link to subscribe, it will work only if you are on your own computer. If the link does not work for some other reason, you will need to follow steps 5 and 6.

 **HOT TIP:** You can often browse the archives of the groups prior to joining. You can also get a sense of how busy the group is by looking at how many emails are sent each month.

# Find and join a Yahoo! group

If you have a Yahoo! email account, you can use your account to find a group of interest to your area of family history research. If you do not have a Yahoo! account, you can still use the site by registering a user name and password with Yahoo!. You can opt to use the group as a mailing list or as a forum, depending on your preference.

**1** Go to http://uk.groups.yahoo.com.

**2** Enter a search term and click Search.

**3** Review your results.

**4** Click Join This Group and you will be taken through the steps to register.

**HOT TIP:** Looking at the number of people the group has gives you an idea of how busy the group may be. Don't be discouraged by small groups though, especially those focused around a surname.

**ALERT:** You may not be approved to join a group immediately. You often have to submit your details and wait for the moderator to send you a note letting you know of your membership status.

# Register with RootsChat forum

This is a very busy forum site devoted primarily to the discussion of family history in the UK and Ireland. There are also several forums dedicated to Commonwealth countries and many native-language forums (Welsh, Gaelic, etc.).

**1** Go to www.rootschat.com.

**2** Click register for free.

**3** Choose a username and enter your details.

**4** Read and type the security code.

**5** Tick I agree after reading the terms and click Register.

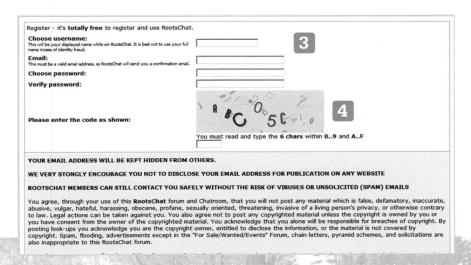

**ALERT:** You will be sent an email with a link after you register. You must click the link from within your email to activate your membership on the forum.

# Find a group on RootsChat forum

You can be a lurker (a person who reads messages but does not post) for as long as you want and while you get a feel for the site. Lurker is not considered a negative term on the Internet. Many people start out this way and join in the discussion as they become more confident writing and responding to posts.

1 Check that you are logged in.

2 Click the Forum tab at the top of the page.

3 Scroll down to a forum area you are interested in.

4 Click a link to view the subforums for that category.

5 Scroll down to the discussion area and click one that you are interested in.

> **! ALERT:** Forums usually contain many subforums. For example, the England forum has individual subforums for most English counties.

| Board name | Topics | Posts | Last post |
|---|---|---|---|
| **Bedfordshire**<br>Ampthill, Bedford, Biggleswade, Hitchin, Leighton Buzzard, Luton, St. Neots, Woburn<br><br>*Child Boards: Bedfordshire Lookup Requests, Bedfordshire Resources & Offers* | 762 | 7527 | **Yesterday at 15:57:03**<br>in Re: The Fooks Family<br>by messy |
| **Berkshire**<br>Abingdon, Basingstoke, Bradfield, Cookham, Easthampstead, Faringdon, Henley, Hungerford, Maidenhead, Newbury, Oxford, Reading, Wallingford, Wantage, Windsor, Witney, Wokingham<br>*Moderator: Little Nell*<br><br>*Child Boards: Berkshire Lookup Requests, Berkshire Resources & Offers* | 1199 | 9995 | **Today at 00:41:42**<br>in Re: 1871 Census - Witney<br>by myancestorsearch |
| **Buckinghamshire**<br>Amersham, Aylesbury, Berkhampstead, Bicester, Brackley, Buckingam, Eton, Headington, Henley, Leighton Buzzard, Newport Pagnell, Potterspury, Thame, Winslow, Wycombe<br><br>*Child Boards: Buckinghamshire Lookup Requests, Buckinghamshire Resources & Offers* | 949 | 5839 | Sunday 08 May 11 18:58 BST (UK)<br>in Re: Richard Bovington bi...<br>by pcpalmer |
| **Cambridgeshire**<br>Cambridge, Caxton, Chesterton, Downham, Ely, Linton, Newmarket, North Witchford, Peterborough, Risbridge, Royston, St. Ives, St. Neots, Whittlesey, Wisbech<br>*Moderator: RootsChat*<br><br>*Child Boards: Cambridgeshire Lookup Requests, Cambridgeshire Resources & Offers* | 927 | 6895 | **Yesterday at 22:52:14**<br>in Re: Baptism look-up plea...<br>by TaraK |
| **Cheshire**<br>Altrincham, Ashton under Lyne, Birkenhead, Bucklow, Chester, Congleton, Great Boughton, Hayfield, High Peak, Macclesfield, Market Drayton, Nantwich, Northwich, Runcorn, Stockport, Warrington, Whitchurch, Wirral, Wrexham<br>*Moderator: JDGen*<br><br>*Child Boards: Cheshire Lookup Offers, Cheshire Lookup Requests, Cheshire Resources* | 2416 | 19666 | **Yesterday at 22:20:48**<br>in Re: Nantwich All Saints ...<br>by marthaannie |
| **Cornwall**<br>Bodmin, Camelford, Falmouth, Helston, Holsworthy, Launceston, Liskeard, Penzance, Plympton St. Mary, Redruth, St. Austell, St. Columb, St. Germans, Isles of Scilly, Stratton, Tavistock, Truro<br>*Moderator: krissejoint*<br><br>*Child Boards: Cornwall Lookup Requests, Cornwall Resources & Offers* | 1112 | 8718 | **Yesterday at 22:56:00**<br>in Re: Bedual Farm Liskeard<br>by cm99 |
| Cumberland | | | |

> **! ALERT:** You can navigate back and forth through the forums by clicking on the branch and leaf symbol on the upper left side of the page.

> **HOT TIP:** You can search the archives of the entire forum by clicking on the Search tab at the top of the webpage.

# Post a message on RootsChat

Once you start reading posts you will come up with questions of your own to post or even helpful replies for other members. Most members on family history forums go out of their way to help, so don't be afraid to post any sort of question that you have.

**1** Check that you are logged in and click Forum at the top of the page.

**2** Go to the forum you want to post in.

**3** Click the new topic tab at the top.

 **HOT TIP:** You can add an emoticon to your message by clicking on one of the yellow smiley faces over the message box.

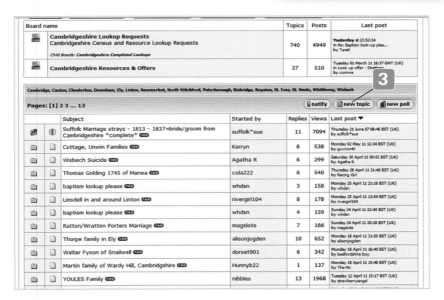

**4** Type a topic in the subject line and type your message in the message box.

**5** Proofread your message and click Post.

**?** **DID YOU KNOW?**
This site alerts you by email when you have received a reply to your post.

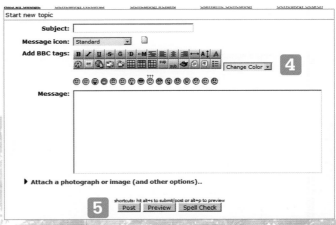

# Search the Rootsweb surname list

You can search through this list to find other family historians researching the same surname as you. People who post their information on this site want to be contacted by others with possible shared ancestry. Most leave contact information in the form of an email address or webpage. While you are browsing, check that the location and other details match the person or people you are researching.

**1** Got to http://rsl.rootsweb.ancestry.com.

**2** Enter a surname.

**3** Click Submit.

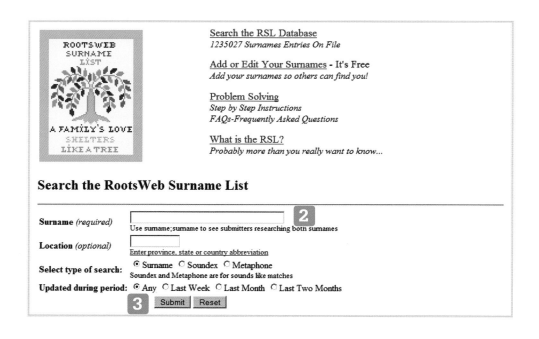

ROOTSWEB
SURNAME
LIST

A FAMILY'S LOVE
SHELTERS
LIKE A TREE

<u>Search the RSL Database</u>
*1235027 Surnames Entries On File*

<u>Add or Edit Your Surnames</u> - It's Free
*Add your surnames so others can find you!*

<u>Problem Solving</u>
*Step by Step Instructions*
*FAQs-Frequently Asked Questions*

<u>What is the RSL?</u>
*Probably more than you really want to know...*

**Search the RootsWeb Surname List**

**Surname** *(required)*    [                    ] **2**
Use surname;surname to see submitters researching both surnames

**Location** *(optional)*    [        ]
Enter province, state or country abbreviation

**Select type of search:**  ⦿ Surname  ○ Soundex  ○ Metaphone
Soundex and Metaphone are for sounds like matches

**Updated during period:**  ⦿ Any  ○ Last Week  ○ Last Month  ○ Last Two Months

**3**  [ Submit ]  [ Reset ]

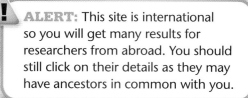

**! ALERT:** This site is international so you will get many results for researchers from abroad. You should still click on their details as they may have ancestors in common with you.

4 Review the results and click Submitter to view the contact details.

5 Note the person's email address so you can contact them directly.

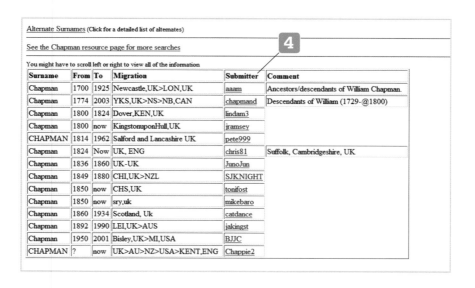

Alternate Surnames (Click for a detailed list of alternates)

See the Chapman resource page for more searches

4

You might have to scroll left or right to view all of the information

| Surname | From | To | Migration | Submitter | Comment |
|---------|------|-----|-----------|-----------|---------|
| Chapman | 1700 | 1925 | Newcastle,UK>LON,UK | aaam | Ancestors/descendants of William Chapman. |
| Chapman | 1774 | 2003 | YKS,UK>NS>NB,CAN | chapmand | Descendants of William (1729-@1800) |
| Chapman | 1800 | 1824 | Dover,KEN,UK | lindam3 | |
| Chapman | 1800 | now | KingstonuponHull,UK | jramsey | |
| CHAPMAN | 1814 | 1962 | Salford and Lancashire UK | pete999 | |
| Chapman | 1824 | Now | UK, ENG | chris81 | Suffolk, Cambridgeshire, UK |
| Chapman | 1836 | 1860 | UK-UK | JunoJun | |
| Chapman | 1849 | 1880 | CHI,UK>NZL | SJKNIGHT | |
| Chapman | 1850 | now | CHS,UK | tonifost | |
| Chapman | 1850 | now | sry,uk | mikebaro | |
| Chapman | 1860 | 1934 | Scotland, Uk | catdance | |
| Chapman | 1892 | 1990 | LEI,UK>AUS | jakingst | |
| Chapman | 1950 | 2001 | Bisley,UK>MI,USA | BJJC | |
| CHAPMAN | ? | now | UK>AU>NZ>USA>KENT,ENG | Chappie2 | |

**HOT TIP:** Try searching by surname only first. If you get too many results, narrow your search by entering the location as well.

# 10 Use DNA testing to support your research

# Introduction

After you do a bit of research and have a well-constructed family tree, you may have unanswered questions about some of your ancestors. This is especially likely when you have a very common surname and can't find your ancestor in the records. DNA testing can help with some of these queries and can also give you a broader understanding of your ethnic background and possible geographic origins.

**ALERT:** DNA genealogy is still a relatively new and evolving field. There have been criticisms levelled against the practice by people concerned with both its accuracy and the ethical implications of what may be discovered (i.e. that a person assumed to be the father is not). At present, there is evidence that paternal line testing yields good results for family history. Less clear is the utility of so-called deep ancestral testing, which suggests your ancient roots. However, as the science matures and as more people participate in DNA testing, the data will become more meaningful.

# Understand Y-DNA and mitochondrial DNA (mtDNA)

Once you have a fleshed-out family tree, take a look at the top and bottom lines of your tree. These are the ones that stretch from you to your father and your father's father, and from you to your mother and all of her direct maternal ancestors. These lines on the tree are the focus of most DNA testing that is currently done.

- Y-DNA: this is the DNA specific to your father and his direct paternal ancestors. On the Y chromosome unique markers are carried directly from father to son through time. It is found only in men.

- mtDNA: this is the DNA in mitochondria which is passed down only through women. Like men, it also carries unique markers specific to her family group. This is found in both men and women.

- Markers: these are slight genetic mutations to the Y-DNA or mtDNA that distinguish people in a family group. These mutations are what scientists look for in DNA testing to establish a relationship between people.

 **ALERT:** You need more than one result to establish a connection between people. The most frequently carried out test is the Y-DNA test to establish a relationship with a surname in the paternal line.

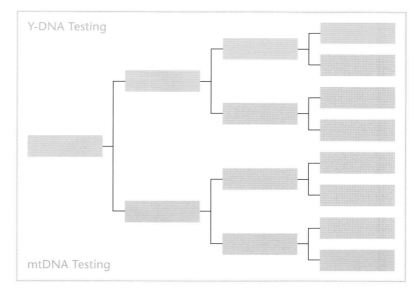

Y-DNA Testing

mtDNA Testing

 **DID YOU KNOW?**
A series of markers is tested to establish relationships. Some of the testing companies may test from 12 to 67 markers and compare them with existing DNA results to find relationships.

 **ALERT:** The type of DNA testing done for family history will not uncover any medical information (e.g. health or disease risk) about you or your family.

# Learn about why to test

If you frequent message boards you may come across an individual whom you believe has an ancestor in common with you. It may be difficult to prove through primary sources but can potentially be proved through genetic testing. This common scenario is only one possible reason for testing. Others include:

- Discover family connections for people who were adopted or whose parentage is uncertain.
- Rule out relationships between people.
- Learn about your possible ethnic or geographic origins.
- Direct your research to a particular geographic area.

**ALERT:** You should have a well-developed question in mind before considering a test.

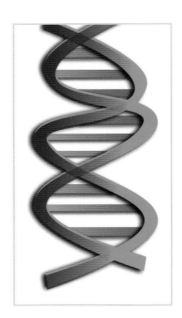

**HOT TIP:** Family surname projects are a good way to get involved in genetic genealogy as you have an established database of people with possible shared ancestry.

**? DID YOU KNOW?**
The DNA test involves a simple swab of your cheek.

# Explore Y-DNA testing options

There are dozens of testing options available to family historians through online testing companies. Different companies will refer to similar tests by different names. Each company has its own unique markers that it reviews. In general, the more markers that are tested for, the more sensitive the results will be and the greater your chances will be of making a connection between individuals. Some specific testing options include:

- Y-DNA markers: a range of markers can be tested (12–67) and used to link you to existing members in the genetic genealogy community.
- Ethnic origins: explore your possible ethnic origins.
- Surname matching: you can be matched with others who share your surname and be given an estimate of how long ago you shared a common relative.
- Ancient ancestry: a test to uncover your most likely geographic origins (or haplogroup).

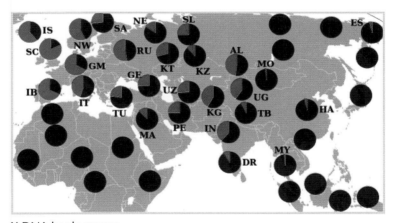

Y-DNA haplogroups

**! ALERT:** Only males can take the Y-DNA tests. If you are a woman, ask a male relative to take the test on your behalf.

**! ALERT:** Your DNA information will be added to the database only with your permission. Adding your information to the database will allow you to make connections with others who share the same genetic markers and possibly family tree.

## WHAT DOES THIS MEAN?
**Haplogroup:** a large group who share a pattern of markers that links them to a common ancestor from ancient times. Most haplogroups are associated with a geographic region.

# Understand mtDNA testing options

Because women's surnames vary so much in a family tree, it is not possible to match genetic results with a surname. In addition, because the markers in mtDNA change much more slowly than in Y-DNA, it is difficult to establish a time frame for relationships. As with commercial Y-DNA tests, companies each have different names for their test but most can:

- Tell you about whether people are related.
- Rule people out of your family tree (i.e. a lack of a genetic match means two or more people are not related).
- Show your possible ethnic origins.
- Be used to identify your haplogroup.

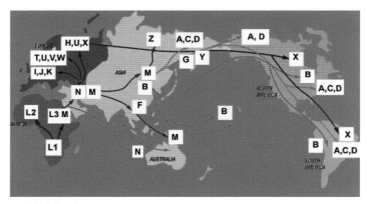

mtDNA haplogroups

**? DID YOU KNOW?**

Either men or women can take mtDNA tests.

**! ALERT:** It's important to understand that the test results for geographic origins are based on statistical probability; they are not certain facts.

# Test for a specific ethnic heritage

While still a new field, you can get some idea of the possibility of being descended from a particular ethnic group. This can be useful if you have a family story of an ancestor who may have come from a different ethnic group. This can be done through mtDNA testing or Y-DNA testing, depending on the reason for your test. Test results for some ethnicities will come back as either positive or negative (Jewish and Native American). Commonly performed heritage tests include:

- Scottish ancestry.
- African ancestry.
- Jewish ancestry.
- Native American ancestry.

 **SEE ALSO:** A DNA project devoted to learning about the relationships among the clans and families of Scotland can be found at www.scottishdna.net.

FamilyTreeDNA
HISTORY UNEARTHED DAILY

Family Tree DNA has

**Discover Your Jewish Ancestry**
Our Jewish comparative databases are the largest in the world, containing records for Ashkenazim and Sephardim, as well as Levites and Cohanim.

ORDER YOUR TEST NOW!

**Family Tree DNA is the pioneer and the world's largest DNA testing company in the new field of genetic genealogy.**

If you are looking for that long-lost relative or ancestor, or if you feel that some day, someone may use a DNA repository to look for long-lost relatives, you should consider doing this simple DNA test.

Your ancestors left clues in your DNA which you can use to determine your deep ancestral origins and to link you with others in recent time. We can compare your results with our database - the largest of its kind in the world - and tell you whether those clues indicate possible Jewish ancestry and whether you match others who are Jewish. Our Jewish comparative databases are the largest in the world, containing records for **Ashkenazim** and **Sephardim**, as well as **Levites** and **Cohanim**.

**Y-DNA:** Males can test their Y-DNA to determine the origin of their paternal line, including the possibility of Jewish and Cohanim ancestry. Note that the Y-DNA strictly checks the paternal line, with no influence from any females along that line. Females do not receive the Y-DNA, and therefore females cannot be tested for the paternal line. If you are a female and would like to know about your paternal line, you would need to have a brother or a male relative from that line to be tested.

 **HOT TIP:** There are many DNA groups through the Family Tree DNA website that link researchers with common heritage from Ireland and Wales.

**SEE ALSO:** There is a website dedicated to tracing Jewish ancestry, including a list of surname projects. You can compare your results to a database of Ashkenazi, Sephardic, Levite and Cohanim Y-DNA at www.jewishgen.org/DNA/genbygen.html.

# Decide who will take the test

Depending on the type of test, you may need to ask a relative to take the test for you. In order to find a suitable candidate, look at your family tree. You may need to look at the collateral lines of your tree (those who are not your parents or grandparents) to find a great uncle, aunt or cousin who is a direct descendant of the person you want to learn about.

- Begin with the ancestor you want to know about.
- Trace a line from that person backwards to a living relative.
- Remember to find a direct male descendant of the person in question for a Y-DNA test.
- Find a direct female descendant of the person for an mtDNA test.

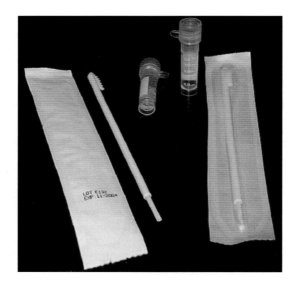

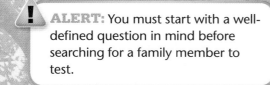 **ALERT:** You must start with a well-defined question in mind before searching for a family member to test.

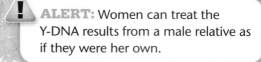 **ALERT:** Women can treat the Y-DNA results from a male relative as if they were her own.

# Understand and use your test results

Most companies will provide you with a visual summary of the markers you tested for, usually presented as a series of numbers in a table. If your markers match those of another person, a relationship is likely. If you and another person tested at the same time, you will receive a summary of both results and the degree of relationship (provided you both agreed to disclose the information to each other).

You can use your results in the following ways:

- Compare your markers with an existing DNA database.
- Upload the information to your Ancestry.co.uk account
- Share your Y-DNA results with a surname project (see next section).

---

**Results:**

Restriction digest with the appropriate enzymes (Figure 1) demonstrated that the sample 2413 corresponded with patterns expected of haplogroup X, indicating maternal Native American ancestry (Table 1).

Table 1. Results of mtDNA testing.

|  | A | B | C | D | X1 | X2 |
|---|---|---|---|---|---|---|
|  | +663 HaeIII | 9 bp deletion | -13259 HincII | -5176 AluI | -1715 DdeI | -10394 DdeI |
| 2413 | negative | negative | negative | negative | positive | positive |

This table displays the five maternal Native American tests, A, B, C, D, and X, that were performed. Below each group designation is a description of specifically what each is testing for. For example, the A test is looking for a site in the mitochondrial DNA (mtDNA) at position 663 where HaeIII, which acts like a pair of molecular scissors, can cut. So a negative test result means that HaeIII did NOT cut. Conversely, in the C test, we look at position 13259 on the mtDNA to see if HincII, another pair of molecular scissors, will NOT cut. So a negative test result means that HincII DID cut.

---

**! ALERT:** A match on a low-resolution test (12 markers) provides evidence of some relationship with another person, but the time frame is less clear.

 **DID YOU KNOW?**
A match on a high-resolution Y-DNA test (67 out of 67 markers) would be expected in father/son/brother relationships.

# Find a surname project

Surname projects are growing rapidly on the Internet and you may be able to join an existing project for the UK or Ireland. Some surname projects may focus on a surname in a specific geographic region. You can find a surname project in the following ways:

- Join the GENEALOGY-DNA mailing list:
  http://lists.rootsweb.com/index/other/DNA/GENEALOGY-DNA.html
- Search through the project names on www.familytreedna.com.
- Use a search engine to find a group. Enter your surname followed by DNA surname project (i.e. Morris DNA surname project).
- Search for a project on www.worldfamilies.net/search.

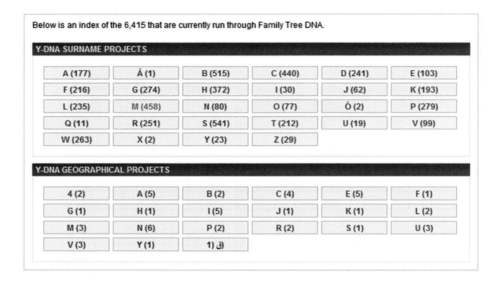

Below is an index of the 6,415 that are currently run through Family Tree DNA.

**Y-DNA SURNAME PROJECTS**

| A (177) | Á (1) | B (515) | C (440) | D (241) | E (103) |
|---|---|---|---|---|---|
| F (216) | G (274) | H (372) | I (30) | J (62) | K (193) |
| L (235) | M (458) | N (80) | O (77) | Ó (2) | P (279) |
| Q (11) | R (251) | S (541) | T (212) | U (19) | V (99) |
| W (263) | X (2) | Y (23) | Z (29) | | |

**Y-DNA GEOGRAPHICAL PROJECTS**

| 4 (2) | A (5) | B (2) | C (4) | E (5) | F (1) |
|---|---|---|---|---|---|
| G (1) | H (1) | I (5) | J (1) | K (1) | L (2) |
| M (3) | N (6) | P (2) | R (2) | S (1) | U (3) |
| V (3) | Y (1) | 1) ﭺ | | | |

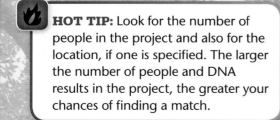

**HOT TIP:** Look for the number of people in the project and also for the location, if one is specified. The larger the number of people and DNA results in the project, the greater your chances of finding a match.

**SEE ALSO:** www.worldfamilies.net also has a large forum of family historians interested in DNA projects. You can browse the message board but must log in to post.

# Join a surname project

Many of the surname projects operate through the testing companies' websites. The advantage of this is that the database is usually held with the company and its search facilities can compare DNA information and analyse relationships. As part of an existing project, you will receive updates when new information is added to the database. Once in a surname project, you can:

- Find living participants who may be related to you.
- Exchange family tree information and research if you have an ancestor in common.
- Learn about possible variations in the spelling of your surname.

**? DID YOU KNOW?**
You can often get a discount on testing if you join an existing surname project through a testing company.

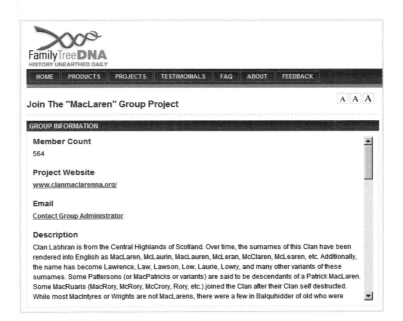

**FamilyTreeDNA**
HISTORY UNEARTHED DAILY

| HOME | PRODUCTS | PROJECTS | TESTIMONIALS | FAQ | ABOUT | FEEDBACK |

**Join The "MacLaren" Group Project**                    A A A

**GROUP INFORMATION**

**Member Count**
564

**Project Website**
www.clanmaclarenna.org/

**Email**
Contact Group Administrator

**Description**
Clan Labhran is from the Central Highlands of Scotland. Over time, the surnames of this Clan have been rendered into English as MacLaren, McLaurin, MacLauren, McLeran, McClaren, McLearen, etc. Additionally, the name has become Lawrence, Law, Lawson, Low, Laurie, Lowry, and many other variants of these surnames. Some Pattersons (or MacPatricks or variants) are said to be descendants of a Patrick MacLaren. Some MacRuaris (MacRory, McRory, McCrory, Rory, etc.) joined the Clan after their Clan self destructed. While most MacIntyres or Wrights are not MacLarens, there were a few in Balquhidder of old who were

**! ALERT:** Most projects will ask you to share information on your earliest known ancestor – the person furthest back in your tree with the surname.

**HOT TIP:** If you already have results from a Y-DNA test, you can share the information with any project by entering the information yourself into their database.

# 11 Continue your search with other sources

# Introduction

The internet is a great place to start your family tree but you will almost certainly need to make use of local sources as you continue your research. There is a real pleasure in viewing old records and scrolling through microfilm to uncover details about your family's history. Travelling to local archives and history societies also provides you with an opportunity to meet other researchers and get help from professionals. You can often use the internet as a starting point for gathering information about these offline sources before you embark on a research trip. Finally, the information presented in this chapter should take you beyond the basic facts of your family history (dates, names, etc.) and help you put your relatives' lives in an historical context.

# Search local records offices

Most counties have records offices which contain collections of great interest to family historians, such as parish registers, non-conformist registers, street directories, workhouse records, and possibly school and hospital records. What you'll find depends on the office. More recently, some offices have started to publish popular records online.

- Search the Internet for your county records office (e.g. Suffolk County Records Office) or the records office where your relative lived.
- Search the website for the types of records available in the office.
- Check for details about what form of identification you need to get a reader's ticket.
- Check on restrictions the office may have against bringing certain items (laptops, cameras, water, etc.).

**HOT TIP:** Many local records offices or archives also contain historical maps and photographs of the area where your relatives lived.

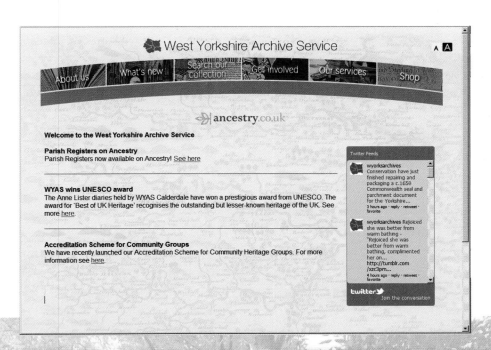

**ALERT:** Offices may be referred to as an archives centre, local history centre or local history collection. Alter your search query if you do not get results searching for a local records office.

**SEE ALSO:** There are large index sites worth exploring as you continue your research, including the popular Cyndi's list at www.cyndislist.com and also the UK-based http://genuki.org.uk.

# Visit LDS family history centres

The LDS has more than 100 centres located throughout the UK. The records vary by site, but most contain a good collection of parish records. Larger centres like the one in London have collections of probate records, property records, court documents and business records. See the link below for a complete list of centres as well as their contact details.

- Find a centre near you at www.lds.org.uk/contact-us/family-history-centres.
- Search or browse the film catalogue at the London centre – www.londonfhc.org – to get an idea of the collections.
- Call your local centre for information about records on site and ask about their operating days and hours.
- Attend a family history presentation at one of the centres.

**ALERT:** You do not have to be a member to use the history centres' resources.

**HOT TIP:** If your local LDS centre does not contain a record you want, you can ask to have that record sent from another centre.

**ALERT:** You must call to check on opening hours or whether you can make an appointment.

# Join a local history society

Some of the best information for your area of research can be found in a local history society. Enthusiasm for local and family history has grown in recent years and many counties, towns and even villages have formed societies to meet the surge in interest. Many societies use mailing lists or forums to keep members up to date.

The benefits of joining a local society inlude:

- Learn about the records available for the area and how to access them.
- Attend regular meetings and presentations.
- Meet others researching a shared surname.
- Receive newsletters with member updates and research tips.

**SEE ALSO:** Scottish Family History societies: www.safhs.org.uk.

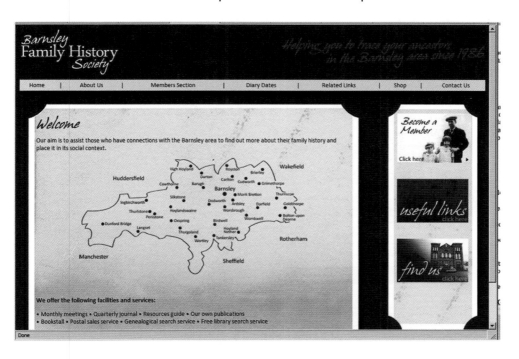

**SEE ALSO:** Search the list of societies on the Federation of Family Historian Societies website: www.ffhs.org.uk/members2/alpha.php for a society near you.

**ALERT:** Most societies will charge a modest annual membership fee.

# Consider joining the Society of Genealogists

The SOG (www.sog.org.uk/index.shtml) is a national institution with a large library in London which holds many records of interest to family historians, including a vast collection of individual family trees. You can join the society or pay a fee each time you use the library or attend one of their courses or lectures.

By joining the SOG you can:

- Gain free access to the London library records.
- Receive the quarterly publication, the *Genealogist Magazine*.
- Join the members' mailing list on Rootsweb.
- Have access to subscription websites from within the library.

**HOT TIP:** Members also receive a discount on subscriptions to FindMyPast.com.

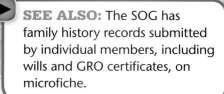

**SEE ALSO:** The SOG has family history records submitted by individual members, including wills and GRO certificates, on microfiche.

# Browse newspaper archives

Old newspapers can be a good source of information about your relatives. If you search through a local or regional paper, you may discover marriage announcements or obituaries, especially towards the end of the 19th century when such postings became common. It is also worth looking in the national papers, many of which have made their archives available online and searchable by keyword.

- Local records offices and larger libraries often have newspapers archived on microfilm or microfiche.
- Connected Histories has British newspapers from 1600–1900, mostly from London – www.connectedhistories.org/resource.aspx?sr=bu.
- *The Times* archives – http://archive.timesonline.co.uk/tol/archive/ – charge a fee to view the digitised pages but all material is fully indexed and searchable.
- 19th Century Serials at www.ncse.ac.uk/index.html is free to search.
- British newspapers 1800–1900 – http://newspapers.bl.uk/blcs/ – is a fee site from the British Library.

 **HOT TIP:** Even if you do not find specific details for your ancestors, browsing through newspaper archives is an excellent way to get a sense of the time and place in which your relatives lived.

# Understand probate records

Wills and letters of administration are some of the most fascinating and useful original sources for the family historian as they contain information about the individual's address, occupation and extended family members. Wills were left by many people in England and Wales, even those of modest means. However, they can also involve the most work to understand and locate. Reviewing the information below on the probate process will help you with your next step: finding copies of probate records for your relative.

- After 1858 wills for England and Wales were proved by the Civil Court of Probate. The court was also responsible for granting letters of administration.
- Copies of wills and administrations were all sent to the Principal Probate Registry in London.

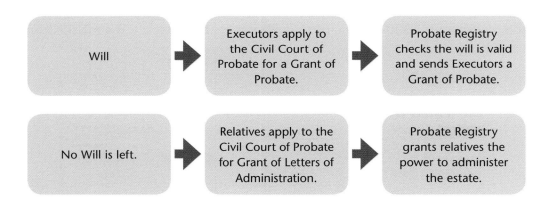

| Will | Executors apply to the Civil Court of Probate for a Grant of Probate. | Probate Registry checks the will is valid and sends Executors a Grant of Probate. |
| No Will is left. | Relatives apply to the Civil Court of Probate for Grant of Letters of Administration. | Probate Registry grants relatives the power to administer the estate. |

**! ALERT:** When you locate a Grant of Probate in the Probate Registry, it usually has a copy of the original will attached.

## WHAT DOES THIS MEAN?

**Grant:** the document issued by the Court of Probate which allowed the money and assets of the deceased to be distributed or sold.

# Find probate records

You can search for grants for all of England and Wales in the National Probate Calendar located at the Principal Probate Registry in London. There are also 11 local registries throughout the UK that hold information for the area concerned. The calendar is organised by the year the grant was issued (not necessarily date of death) and by surname.

**1** Search the Probate Calendar at the Principal Probate Registry or at a local registry for your ancestor.

**2** Check the index (National Probate Calendar 1861–1941) on Ancestry.co.uk if you have an account.

**3** Order a copy of a grant from the Principal Probate Registry in London or a local registry.

> **SEE ALSO:** Records for Scotland are held at the National Archives of Scotland and can be searched for free on http://scotlandspeople.gov.uk/.

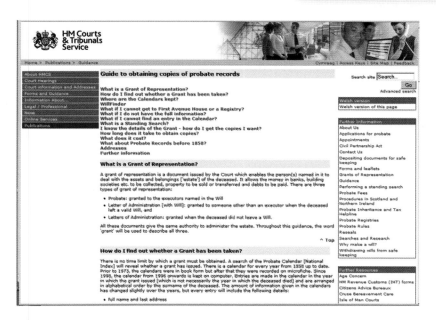

**HOT TIP:** You can pay to get a registry to search for a grant for you. However, you *must* send the request in writing by following the instructions here: www.hmcourts-service.gov.uk/cms/1226.htm#addresses. (Look under What if I cannot get to First Avenue House or a Registry?)

**DID YOU KNOW?** Prior to 1882, a married woman needed her husband's permission to make a will.

# Explore social history resources

During your research you might come across some obsolete occupation or trade names, or you may have learned that your relative lived in a workhouse or was the resident of a village that no longer exists. Time spent researching the social history of the era in which your relatives lived will give you an appreciation of what their daily lives were like and also provide you with a window into the history of the UK.

- Search the index of old occupations at www.familyresearcher.co.uk/glossary/Dictionary-of-Old-Occupations-Index.html.
- Explore the Vision of Britain site for maps and historical statistics of the place you are interested in – www.visionofbritain.org.uk.
- Gain a better understanding of UK history at the Institute of Historical Research site – www.british-history.ac.uk.
- Read about the creation and growth of workhouses in the 19th century on the excellent www.workhouses.org.uk site.
- Explore Victorian social history at www.victorianweb.org/history/sochistov.html.
- Search through the primary resources on London Lives www.londonlives.org.

**HOT TIP:** Use some of these websites to research the place your ancestors came from if you are unable to travel to the area or the local records offices.

**ALERT:** The London Lives website has a superb collection of resources online, including records from parish, criminal, coroner and hospital archives in London from 1690 to 1800. The records are all searchable by name or keyword.

# Top 10 Online Research Problems Solved

# Problem 1: I can't find a file I downloaded

If you forget to save a file from one of the family history sites but think you downloaded it, you can usually find it on your computer in the Downloads file.

**1** Click Start and select the top folder on the right (whatever your computer is named).

**2** Double-click on the Downloads File Folder.

**3** Scan the files for the one you are looking for.

**4** Open the document and save it in a location you are likely to remember.

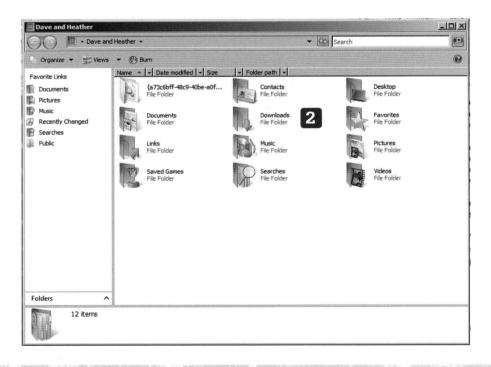

**HOT TIP:** You can click on the Date modified tab at the top of the Downloads folder to sort the files by date.

# Problem 2: I've lost a file I saved

You can perform a search on your computer to find a file or folder that you've lost, even if you don't remember the entire file name.

**1** Click the Start menu.

**2** Type the file name or key word into the field.

**3** A list of potential matches will appear over the search field.

**4** Click and open the file and save it to a location you will remember.

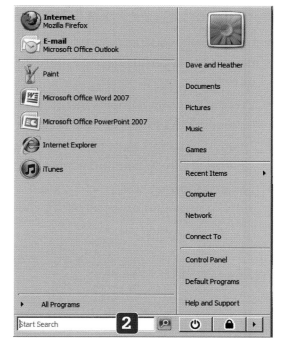

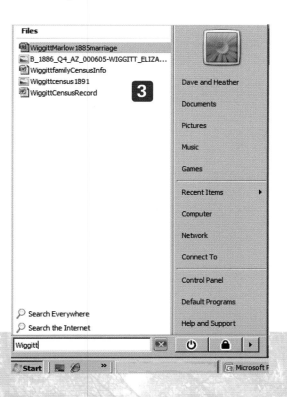

> **HOT TIP:** You can enter part of the file name if you don't remember the exact name.

# Problem 3: I have conflicting information for my ancestor

You may end up with several potential birth, marriage and death dates for your relative and even a variety of occupations. This is not uncommon and does not mean that all the information you have is incorrect, though some of it probably is. Keep the following in mind when you are trying to piece together evidence for your relative:

- Use primary sources when deciding something is an historical fact. In other words, do not rely on a census form or marriage certificate as evidence of a person's birth place or date.

- Understand that some of the official records contain errors or that your ancestor may have reported their information incorrectly – sometimes knowingly.

- Treat information from other researchers or even from family members with some caution until you can find evidence for the facts yourself.

- Understand that people changed occupations over their lifetime, especially in the 19th century and especially if they were working class.

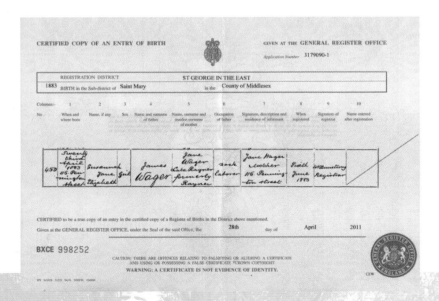

**DID YOU KNOW?**

One of the most common problems on census forms is the misspelling of individuals' names.

# Problem 4: I can't find information for a particular ancestor

There will always be one or more ancestors whose existence in the sources seems to elude you. Family historians refer to them as brick wall ancestors. Use the strategies below to help guide your search for the relative in question.

- Go back through your references and rethink the information you have. You may have a minor detail wrong about their dates, name or location.
- Vary the spelling of their name and also widen the date ranges for them to include more than five years.
- Search for their records on more than one site.
- Do a census search with their sibling's name to try to locate them.
- Ask for help from other researchers on a family history mailing list, forum or local history society.
- Take your search offline and visit your local records office, family history centre or library.

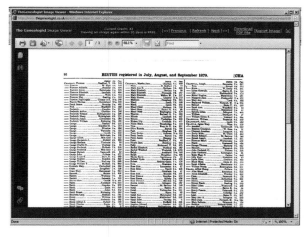

© Crown Copyright. Image reproduced by courtesy of the controller of HMSO and the Office for National Statistics via www.TheGenealogist.co.uk

 **ALERT:** If the information about your relative is from another researcher, always check their sources and draw your own conclusions about the data.

 **HOT TIP:** Search for the relative using their middle name. Sometimes mistakes are made transcribing indexes onto websites.

# Problem 5: I'm having difficulty printing a record image

Some records are difficult to print out because of their shape, orientation and amount of information on them. You can alter your print properties to get the results you want.

**1** Click Print on an image you want.

**2** Click Properties when the print dialogue box appears.

**3** Click the Finishing tab to change the orientation (for census records especially).

Or

**4** Click Effects and select % of Normal Size.

**5** Enter a number value to reduce or enlarge the image.

**6** Click OK and print.

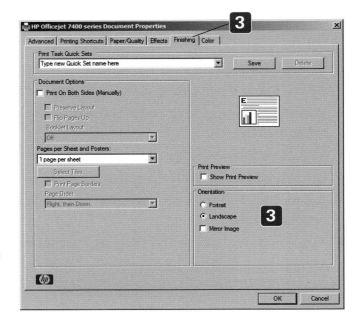

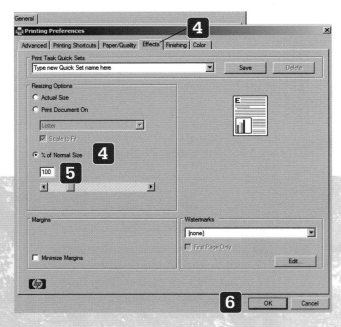

**HOT TIP:** You can also slide the bar beneath the number field to alter the image size.

# Problem 6: I have forgotten my username or password

It is not uncommon to forget your username or password, particularly if you have not visited a site for a while. Most websites are able to remember your email address and once you enter your information, they can email you your user name, password or both.

For Ancestry.co.uk:

**1** Click Forgot Username/Password at the top of the page.

**2** Enter your email address and click Request Login Information.

**3** Check your email for your login information.

Forgot Your Username or Password?

Please enter the email address from your Ancestry.co.uk account below. We'll send you an email with your username and instructions for creating a new password or changing your username.

Be sure to check your junk or spam folder if you don't receive our email soon.

**Email Address:**

Request Login Information **2**

NEED HELP?

How to retrieve or change your Ancestry password

Why links for a forgotten username or password may not work

 **ALERT:** You may have to use a temporary password and then choose a different one. Be sure to write down the new password in a safe location.

 **HOT TIP:** You can use your email address as your username on both Ancestry.co.uk and findmypast.co.uk if you remember your password.

For findmypast.co.uk:

**4** Click Sign In at the top of the page.

**5** Click Forgotten Password?

**6** Enter your email and click Send password.

**7** Check your email for your password information.

# Problem 7: I'm receiving too many emails from my subscription site

You can inadvertently sign up to receive multiple emails and other solicitations from the subscription site you joined. You have control over what you receive in your inbox and can opt not to receive any mail.

For ancestry.co.uk:

**1** Check that you are signed in and click My Account.

**2** Click Update your email preferences.

**3** Tick or untick the types of updates you want to receive.

**4** Click Update Preferences.

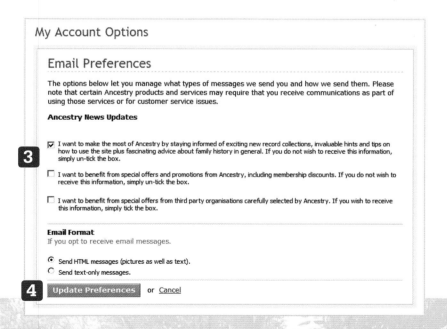

**ALERT:** Consider receiving some of the updates from the site as they will inform you of newly added records as well as useful shortcuts and tips for researching your family history.

For findmypast.co.uk:

**5** Check that you are signed in and then click Manage My Account.

**6** Click My personal details.

**7** Untick the box under preferences for receiving marketing information.

**8** Click Update my details.

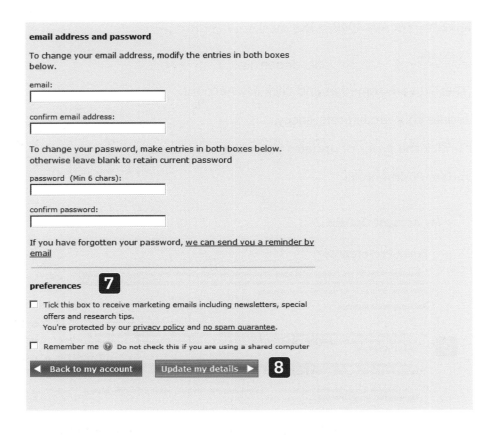

# Problem 8: I'm receiving too many emails from my mailing list

Some family history groups are very active and individual emails can clog up your inbox quickly. You can alter the settings of your membership in most groups and opt to receive a digest or choose to read the messages on the web only.

**1** Click on your profile or account, depending on the site.

**2** Click notification and/or email.

**3** Select the types of emails or notifications that you want to receive (i.e. daily digest).

**4** Click Save (or Save settings).

**WHAT DOES THIS MEAN?**

A digest is a group of messages (posts) from a mailing list contained in one email.

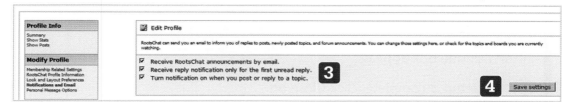

For Yahoo! Groups:

**5** Check that you are signed into your Yahoo! account.

**6** Go to My groups and click on your mailing group.

**7** Click Edit membership at the top of the page.

**8** Under step 2, select your message preference and click Save Changes.

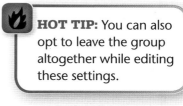

**HOT TIP:** You can also opt to leave the group altogether while editing these settings.

# Problem 9: I'm having trouble viewing the documents on ancestry.co.uk

You may have difficulty viewing the digitised records or navigating around the record to see all the information. Ancestry offers an enhanced viewer option that you can download to your computer for free.

**1** Click on an image to view and you should be prompted to download the viewer.

**2** When you are prompted, click Yes, download it now.

**3** When the download box appears, click Run.

**4** Click Yes when the User Account control dialogue box appears.

**5** When the setup is complete, click Close on the setup box.

If you are not prompted to download the viewer:

a. While in image view, click Option and select Use Enhanced Images.

b. Follow the steps above to download the viewer.

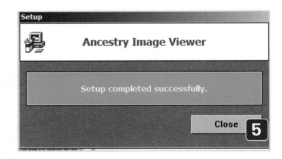

**ALERT:** Depending on your security settings and browser, you may have to click Allow to download the program or click on the bar at the top of your screen to permit the program to continue.

# Problem 10: The images on findmypast.co.uk are slow to download

The website has an optional enhanced image viewer that is free to download. It takes just a minute to download to your computer using the following steps:

**1** While viewing an image, click Download free enhanced image viewer.

**2** Choose the version for your computer and click Download.

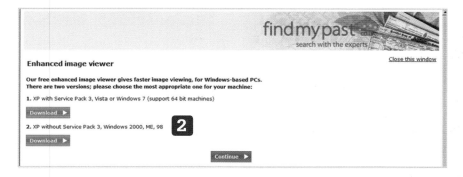

**3** Click Run or open when the download box appears.

**4** After the viewer is installed, click Continue.

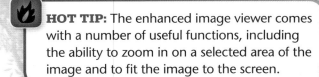

**HOT TIP:** The enhanced image viewer comes with a number of useful functions, including the ability to zoom in on a selected area of the image and to fit the image to the screen.

# Also available in the In Simple Steps series

Laptop Basics
Windows 7 Edition

9780273736806

Computer Basics
Windows 7 edition

9780273736844

Windows 7

9780273729136

Editing, Storing & Sharing Digital Photos

9780273744146

Using the Internet for the Over 50s

9780273734932

Build your First Website

9780273745419

Computer Basics for the Over 50s

9780273729174

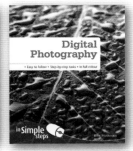

Digital Photography

9780273723516

Scanning and Restoring your Old Photos

9780273762591

Social Networking for the Over 50s

9780273761075

Computer Problems Solved for the Over 50s

9780273746355

Windows 7 for the Over 50s

9780273729181

Branch | D
CN | i/1

in Simple steps